MARTY
PREACHER

John Peters

EXETER
THE PATERNOSTER PRESS

AUSTRALIA
Bookhouse Australia Ltd.,
P.O. Box 115, Flemington Markets,
N.S.W. 2129.

SOUTH AFRICA
Oxford University Press,
P.O. Box 1141, Cape Town.

British Library Cataloguing in Publication Data

Peters, John
  Martyn Lloyd-Jones, preacher.
  1. Lloyd-Jones, D.M.   2. Methodist Church
  (*Great Britain*) — Biography   3. Physicians
  — Wales — Biography
  I. Title
  280'.4 BX 8495.L5/

ISBN 0-85364-416-0

Typeset by Busby's Typesetting & Design, Exeter, Devon
and Printed in Great Britain for The Paternoster Press,
Paternoster House, 3 Mount Radford Crescent, Exeter, Devon
by Cox & Wyman, Reading.

CONTENTS

Cover Photograph **Desmond Groves** F.B.I.P.P., F.R.P.S., F.R.S.A.

FOREWORD

When, a couple of years ago, a young man 'phoned me one evening and said that he was proposing to write a book about my husband, I am afraid that I was not very encouraging. Iain Murray's official biography was about to appear; Christopher Catherwood, our eldest grandson, was thinking out a shorter appreciation to be included in his *Five Evangelical Leaders*. What could this young man, who did not even know him personally, have to add to what was already written? There is no doubt about it, I was downright discouraging.

But I was wrong, and I am glad that John Peters was not going to be put off by my somewhat unenthusiastic acceptance of his determination to write. For this is a good book, and I am happy to give it my warm commendation — and the family is in complete agreement with me. The author is not afraid to report the criticisms of MLl-J as well as the praises, while his own opinions are quite obvious. His familiarity with the books themselves has amazed me, and his comments and annotations are copious and useful.

I very much enjoyed reading this book, and I pray that this may be the experience of many.

May the Lord greatly bless both the book and its author, and use it to His glory.

BETHAN LLOYD-JONES

PREFACE AND ACKNOWLEDGEMENTS

Two of the most formative influences upon my understanding of the Christian faith during the past twenty years have been C.S. Lewis and Dr. Martyn Lloyd-Jones. My debt to the former was set out in *C.S. Lewis: The Man and His Achievement*, published by the Paternoster Press in October 1985. I am now glad to be able to assess the precise nature of the latter's appeal. I am grateful for the use of quotations to publishers of books by Dr. Martyn Lloyd-Jones : Banner of Truth, Evangelical Press of Wales, Hodder and Stoughton, Inter-Varsity Press, Kingsway Publications and Marshall Pickering.

In working on this book I have been helped by a large number of people, many of whom gave freely of their time when I sought interviews with them. Not all of them can be thanked by name, so I will confine my acknowledgements to: Mrs. Lloyd-Jones, who generously agreed to write a Foreword; the Rev. Vernon Higham, who spent a whole morning with me in Cardiff and also lent me several important articles; Peter Cousins, who guided an inexperienced author through the complexities of book publishing; and lastly, to my wife Elisabeth and our children (Daniel, Katherine, and Joanna) for their constant encouragement, especially when the writing was going through a sticky patch. They got used to seeing me disappear into another room to work, and I hope they feel that their sacrifice was worthwhile.

JOHN PETERS

TABLE OF IMPORTANT DATES

1899: *20 December*, born in Cardiff, South Wales, the middle son of three.

1906: *Spring*, moved to Llangeitho, near Cardiganshire, now Dyfed.

1908: *December*, his first visit to London.

1911: Entered Tregaron County School.

1914: *October*, the Lloyd-Jones family moved to London and settled at 7, Regency Street, Westminster.

1916: Started as a medical student at St. Bartholomew's Hospital. Mrs. Lloyd-Jones commenced her studies the same day but at University College, London.

1921: Took his M.R.C.S. and L.R.C.P. degrees in July, followed by his M.B., B.S. degrees in October. In the same year he became Horder's Junior House Physician.

1923: Took his M.D. and subsequently became Clinical Assistant to Horder.

1925: Became M.R.C.P., with a successful career in medicine apparently ahead of him.

1926: *11 November*, preached his first sermon in Wales at Newport, formerly Monmouthshire, now Gwent.
28 November, preached his first sermon at Bethlehem

Forward Movement (Sandfields), Aberavon, South Wales; on 1 Cor. 2:9 (morning) and 1 Cor. 2:2 (evening).

12 December, preached again at Sandfields, this time accompanied by his fiancee, Bethan Phillips. This was the first time she heard him preach.

20 December, official offer of pastorate at Sandfields sent to him by the Secretary, E.T. Rees.

1927: *8 January*, married Bethan Phillips at Charing Cross Chapel, London.

1 February, arrived in Aberavon, after a honeymoon spent in Torquay.

November, their first daughter, Elizabeth, was born.

1932: First visit to America.

1937: Second daughter, Ann was born.

1938: *1 May*, announced his resignation from the pastorate at Sandfields. In the same month he accepted Dr. Campbell Morgan's offer to share the pulpit at Westminster Chapel for an initial period of six months. *July*, left Aberavon.

1939: *April*, accepted the call to a full-time pastorate at Westminster Chapel. During the war the Lloyd-Jones family lived in Haslemere, Surrey (1939–43).

1943: Dr. Campbell Morgan retired, leaving MLl-J as the sole Pastor of the chapel.

1968: Retired from Westminster Chapel.

1969: Delivered a series of lectures at Westminster Theological Seminary, U.S.A., later to be published as *Preaching and Preachers* (1971).

1979-81: Increasing illness. Preached his last sermon at the opening of Barcombe Baptist Chapel *8 June 1980*.

1981: *1 March*, died peacefully in his sleep.

6 March, buried in Newcastle Emlyn, Dyfed.

6 April, Thanksgiving Service at Westminster Chapel.

1982: First volume of the official biography of his life, by Iain Murray, published as *D. Martyn Lloyd-Jones: The First Forty Years 1899–1939*. The second volume will deal with the years down to 1981.

The Lloyd-Jones Family Tree

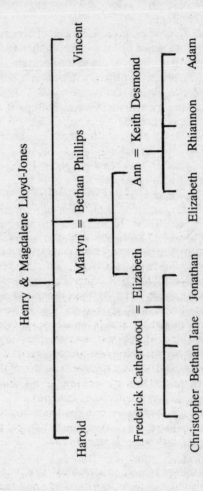

CHAPTER 1

Introduction

Dr. David Martyn Lloyd-Jones died on St. David's Day (1 March) 1981, exactly thirteen years after conducting his last service as minister of Westminster Chapel, when he had preached on Romans 14:17. He had been a preacher for more than fifty years. The word 'preacher' is appropriate, because that is how he would have described himself. It was the role he was sure God had called him to and for which, he was sure, God had equipped him. Preaching, he believed, was 'the most urgent need in the church'[1] as well as being 'the greatest need of the world'.[2] He gave himself to it without reserve. The role of the preacher was one which thrilled him at every level of his being, involving his entire personality, intellect and energies.

His attitude may be seen in the letter he wrote on 30 May 1968, telling members of Westminster Chapel that he intended to retire the following September:

> What things we have experienced! To a preacher nothing is so wonderful as to feel the unction of the Holy Spirit while preaching, and to hear of souls being brought under conviction of sin, and then experiencing the new birth. Thank God, that has often been our experience.[3]

His death deprived the evangelical world of one of its most authoritative, powerful and disciplined leaders. He had been associated with two churches, in Wales and Central London. But the influence he exercised extended throughout the world. People with a historical perspective sometimes described him as the 'last of the preachers', while others saw him as an 'apostle of the twentieth century'. But he saw his role as carrying out the primary task of the church: preaching and expounding the word of God.

Not surprisingly, many people disagreed with him. For much of his life he was, in a sense, an isolated figure; and at times he was involved in controversy,[4] as he held out against many of the theological fashions of the day. Yet to countless thousands of Christians throughout the world, of differing temperaments and denominational tendencies, he had been a source of comfort, encouragement and strength.

He may even have been conscious of the gap that his death would leave. But he had a deep conviction of the continuity of God's grace in each and every generation. One observer, the Revd. Graham Harrison, believes that M. Ll-J sought to remind the Westminster Fellowship (a group of like-minded ministers) of this truth several years before his own death:

> Just a few years ago — before his declining health was to ensure that he was absent from the Westminster Fellowship for extended periods — he told us a story. Some of us felt at the time that there was a strange significance about it. In retrospect I am utterly convinced that he knew what he was doing and that he did it deliberately. It concerned Ebenezer Morris, the great Calvinistic Methodist exhorter (and later minister) at the end of the 18th and during the first quarter of the 19th centuries. He had been ill and it was feared that his departure was at hand. Men in great distress and apprehension came to visit him, fearful for the future. But he was raised up and preached a sermon. His text: Hebrews 8:1 — 'Now of the things which we have spoken this is the sum: *We have such*

an High Priest' . . . 'Don't be worried about when I am gone', said Ebenezer Morris — *'We have such an High Priest.'* And he asked them what the task of the high priest was in the Old Testament. Then he gave them the answer: to keep the fire alight on the altar, and to keep the lamp continually burning.[5]

Volume One of the official biography of his life — dealing with the years 1899—1939 — has already been published.[6] Iain Murray, in an elegant and scholarly way, has chronicled M.Ll-J's story to the end of his first year at Westminster Chapel. The eargerly awaited second volume — dealing with the years 1940—81 — will complete a fitting memorial to a spiritual giant. For some, however, the scope of the whole project (the first volume ran to almost 400 pages and the second is likely to be just as lengthy) may be inhibiting, though less so than the immense volumes on Whitefield written by Arnold Dallimore. So one bleak day in January 1984 I started to write an article on 'the Doctor'[7] which would pin-point, *for ordinary readers like myself*, the importance and significance of his long career, as well as indicating the strengthening effect of his published sermons, most of which appeared after his retirement from Westminster Chapel. This article eventually grew into a more extended work. Already readers will be aware that my main motivation is gratitude to M.Ll-J: he has been one of the formative influences on my understanding, thinking, and appreciation of the 'glorious gospel'. It is a gratitude which became more individual and personal for me eleven years ago, and thus a whole decade before embarking on this volume. I had written to him expressing my thanks for his published sermons on Romans 6. I did not expect a reply from him. Almost by return of post, however, I received the following courteous (not to say treasured) reply:

I must send you just a word to thank you for your most kind and encouraging letter. It warmed my heart and has encouraged me to go on with this work of producing these books.

I am already correcting the next volume on Romans, which will be Chapter 7, and I hope that another volume on Ephesians will also come out this year.

May God greatly bless you in all your ways.[8]

Inevitably certain parts of my work will cover some of the ground already dealt with so capably by Iain Murray, though not in anything like his biographical depth (for that is in any case not my prime concern). For this I ask for the indulgence and patience of my readers. But of necessity my appreciation must begin, if only for the sake of balance, with an account of M.Ll-J's life and career.

CHAPTER 2

An Account of M.Ll-J's Life

When he died at the age of eighty-one M.Ll-J had lived through some of the most momentous and dramatic years in Britain's history: the post-Victorian and Edwardian eras; the constitutional upheaval caused by the abdication of Edward VIII at the end of 1936; two World Wars, with all the horrific loss of life that is inevitably a part of global fighting; the grimness of unemployment in the 1930s and the post-1945 austerity; the decline in church attendance and organized religion in general; later, the spread of pornography and the casual acceptance of lax, indeed immoral standards; the philosophy of pessimism; the ever-increasing numbers of people seeking divorce; and the inability of churchmen and politicians to provide a solution to Britain's moral degeneration.

'The Doctor' had, by any standards, a very long life. It spanned the last two years of Victoria's reign (her dates as Queen were from 1837–1901), the whole of the reigns of Edward VII (1901–10), George V (1910–36), Edward VIII (1936), George VI (1936–52), and twenty-nine years of the reign of Elizabeth II (from 1952 onwards).

Put another way, he had witnessed the political fortunes of

as many as eighteen Prime Ministers,[1] some of whom were in office on more than one occasion — for example, Stanley Baldwin, Ramsay Macdonald, Winston Churchill, and Harold Wilson.

In the last twenty years of his life, too, there had been an enormous increase in the cult of the 'super-star' in the world of the cinema and sport: witness the popularity of the Beatles; the huge salaries paid to footballers, cricketers, and television stars; and an increasingly intrusive interest in the lives of those considered to be 'public property' — particularly the members of the Royal Family and leading politicians.

In contrast to all of this, MLl-J disliked intensely the cult of the personality; so much so that it was only in the last year of his life that he co-operated fully with his biographer, and then largely at the insistence of his family.[2] When he died, surrounded by a family who both loved and respected him, he was very much the 'Grand Old Man' of evangelicalism whose published sermons — mostly brought out in his retirement — sold in large numbers each year.[3]

EARLY YEARS

How did it all come about? For the start of his story we must go back to the closing year of the nineteenth century; in fact to 20 December 1899, when he was born in Donald Street, Cardiff, South Wales. He was the middle child of three sons born to Henry and Magdalene (known as Maggie) Lloyd-Jones. His father was a Congregationalist, then a Calvinistic Methodist, and a Liberal by political persuasion; whereas his mother, a Tory voter, was attached to the Church of England as a result of her upbringing.

In later life, MLl-J recalled very little of his life in Wales's largest city. This was in total contrast to the comprehensive richness and variety of his recollections of Llangeitho, Cardiganshire (now Dyfed), whither the family had moved in the spring of 1906. Whereas Cardiff was a bustling, cosmopolitan, largely English-speaking place, Llangeitho was rural, isolated, old-fashioned, largely Welsh-speaking and religious. But, as he said himself in later years, it was a particular brand of religion:

> While large congregations still met to worship on Sundays, morning and evening, it was the strong sense of tradition which accounted for it. Llangeitho had lost the fire and the rejoicing of the Methodist Revival to the same extent as Westminster Abbey had lost the life and vitality of the Early Church — "The glory had departed from Israel".[4]

At this time he was extremely happy and fulfilled, but this contented state of mind was to change when he entered the County School in the market town of Tregaron, four miles from Llangeitho, after being placed second in the 1911 scholarship examination. Intellectually he matured a great deal there, and developed a keen interest in history. Emotionally, however, he was afflicted by that particular form of homesickness called in Welsh *hiraeth* and from which he was to suffer in later life when away from his home and family.

In 1914, his father's financial affairs took a decided turn for the worst. By October the family had transferred to London, setting up home at 7, Regency Terrace, Westminster, and naturally hoping for an upturn in their fortunes.

Two years later he enrolled as a medical student in one of Britain's finest and most famous teaching hospitals, St. Bartholomew's (commonly referred to as 'Bart's'). From then on, with the exception of the eleven and a half years he spent in Aberavon, London was to be his home, even after retiring from Westminster Chapel.

, Clearly in his element at Bart's, MLl-J took his M.R.C.S. and L.R.C.P. in July 1921, followed by his M.B.B.S. in October of the same year. In 1921 he also began to work as a Junior House Physician for Sir Thomas Horder, one of Bart's most distinguished and brilliant men.[5] Horder made strenuous demands on his staff, as MLl-J soon found out:

> There was one occasion, for example, when Sir Thomas

was so late in preparing the material for some important
public lectures which he was giving, that Lloyd-Jones and
another junior member of staff had to have permission to
remain in the Bart's Library late into the night pursuing
quotations and references which would be needed the next
day. The work was not completed before the research
colleague collapsed with exhaustion and had to be removed
to a ward where Lloyd-Jones revived him with brandy![6]

In his twenties he was academically successful, with excellent
prospects. But this period of his life was notable for a radical
change in his attitude and response to Christianity. This is how
he described it, many years later:

> For many years I thought I was a Christian when in fact
> I was not. It was only later that I came to see that I had
> never been a Christian and became one. But I was a
> member of a church and attended my church and its
> services regularly. So anybody assuming, as most
> preachers did, that I was a Christian was making a false
> assumption. It was not a true assessment of my condition.
> What I needed was preaching that would convict me of
> sin and make me see my need, and bring me to true
> repentance and tell me something about regeneration. But
> I never heard that. The preaching we had was always based
> on the assumption that we were all Christians, that we
> would not have been there in the congregation unless we
> were Christians. This, I think, has been one of the cardinal
> errors of the Church especially in this present century.[7]

Conviction of sin came gradually, in addition to which he felt
pursued by what Francis Thompson has graphically described
as the 'Hound of Heaven' (a poem MLl-J was to quote frequently
in his sermons). By 1925 a more pressing motivation than
medicine was influencing his whole outlook and thinking: 'He
knew that the same grace which had come to him could bring
people everywhere to real christianity'.[8] The call to the ministry
was now being made effectual in his life. Years later, in chapter

6 of *Preaching and Preachers*, he dealt at some length with the preacher's 'call'. He rejected absolutely the idea that a Chrisian should become a preacher because he has decided to 'take up preaching as a calling' (p.103). His justification for this view is based not just on the fact that it is a misunderstanding and misrepresentation of the biblical teaching, but is based also on the evidence of the lives of great preachers throughout history.

Typically and analytically, he said, certain tests enable a person to determine whether he has a call or not (as opposed to a calling) to preach. He saw it as beginning with what he describes as an 'awareness of a kind of pressure being brought to bear upon one's own spirit . . . some disturbance in the realm of the Spirit' (p.104). It is a consistent and constant God-given pressure and influence.

Whereas the first test is an inward one, the second is external, and generally takes the form of other people suggesting that a person should think of becoming a preacher. This in turn leads to a personal concern for other people, particularly a realization of the true state and condition of people who have not experienced God's salvation.

The most crucial tests of all are what might be termed an irresistible constraint − 'The only man who is called to preach is the man who cannot do anything else' (p.105) − and, equally important, a feeling of unworthiness (cp. 2 Corinthians 2:16)[9] or inadequacy. He summed up his convictions by saying that the man who is 'called' by God is a man who realises what he is called to do, and he so realises the awfulness of the task that he shrinks from it. Nothing but this overwhelming sense of being called, and of compulsion, should ever lead anyone to preach' (p.107).

These factors are easily demonstrated from his own life. But to assume that it was a comparatively easy matter for him to give up medicine would be completely wrong. Indeed, the spiritual and mental struggle involved led directly to considerable loss of weight. By the summer of 1926, however, the whole matter had been resolved, and he was sure in his own mind that henceforth he should become a preacher. Confirmation of the divine nature of his call came, in an unexpected though decisive way, in the autumn of 1926:

One day as he was crossing the Square at Bart's, Geoffrey
Evans, the Assistant Professor of Medicine, stopped and
asked him to 'spare a moment'. Evans disclosed that his
part-time post (which he combined with being a consultant
physician) was becoming vacant and that it was almost
certain that Lloyd-Jones would be approached and offered
the job. It was a position which would have led right to
the top. 'This did not shake me for a second,' Dr. Lloyd-
Jones was later to comment, 'I had already decided for
the ministry'.[10]

In the same year he became engaged to Bethan Phillips
(eighteen months older than himself), whose influence on his
life was to be profound. Her father, Dr. Tom Phillips, was a native
of Newcastle Emlyn, where her grandfather, the Revd. Evan
Phillips, had been minister of Bethel Calvinistic Methodist
Chapel for more than fifty years, and where MLl-J was himself
to be buried fifty-five years later. Also a medical student, she
obtained the degrees of M.R.C.S., L.R.C.P. and Bachelor of
Surgery. She heard him preach for the first time on Sunday 12
December 1926, and they were married on 8 January 1927. They
set up their first home together at 57, Victoria Terrace, Aberavon.
Their two daughters, Elizabeth and Ann, were both born during
'the Doctor's' pastorate in South Wales, Elizabeth in 1927 (though
she was actually born in London owing to medical complica-
tions), and Ann ten years later.

As far as Mrs. Lloyd-Jones's own spiritual experience was
concerned, she has placed on record the following important
piece of information in *Memories of Sandfields*:

> In those early years at Aberavon, I rejoiced to see men
> and women converted – drunkards, evil-livers – all
> manner of types and backgrounds *and* all different ages!
> I rejoiced to see them and I envied them and sometimes
> wished, when I saw their radiant faces and changed lives,
> that I had been a drunkard or worse, so that I could be
> converted! I never imagined that *I* needed to be converted,
> having always been a 'Christian' or that I could get any

more than I had already! In those first two years, God graciously used Martyn's morning sermons to open my eyes and to show me myself and my needs. I came to know my sins forgiven and the peace of God in my heart.[11]

ABERAVON

MLl-J was offered the pastorate of Sandfields on 20 December 1926. His salary was to be £225 per annum, plus manse and rates, with thirteen free Sundays each year. It was hardly a princely proposition for someone with his salary prospects in medicine: even in the 1920s a family doctor could expect to earn about £1,500 per annum, while a consultant might receive from £3,500 to £5,000. But his prime interest was not — and never was — financial. Rather he was determined to know neither anything nor anybody among them 'save Jesus Christ and him crucified', which was his text on Sunday 28 November 1926 when he first preached at Aberavon. It is the text on his simple grave in Newcastle Emlyn.

Full-blooded preaching

The next eleven and a half years were memorable, even momentous, for the life of Bethlehem Forward Movement Church, popularly known as 'Sandfields'. This was not due to the new or original methods he adopted[12], but rather to the full-blooded fearless nature of his preaching. It was not emotional (like that of many other preachers in Wales at this time), intellectual or pretentious, nor was it designed primarily to increase the size of the church. It was powerful, biblical, uncompromising, and evangelistic. The flavour and urgency of his sermons at this period are obvious from a perusal of the *Evangelistic Sermons at Aberavon*. Here is part of his conclusion to a sermon entitled 'Man's Fundamental Problem':

Let us honestly face ourselves. Such are our natures. They
love the darkness, they hate the light. They are twisted,
they are perverted, they prefer the wrong to the right and
enjoy evil rather than known good. What we need is not
more light, but a nature which will be capable of loving
the light instead of hating it. The light is there, we know
it to be there but we dislike it. We hate it. What is the
point of hoping vaguely and theoretically for some
supposed additional light, when we cannot appreciate and
enjoy the light we already have? What we need is not
knowledge, but love. We know what is right and good but
we fail to do it because our natures are such that we do
not love it. All the knowledge, culture, and training of the
whole world can never change the nature, can never teach
us how to love God. Try your best and utmost to do so.
In the name of this gospel I defy you to succeed. But do
not be so foolish, do not be so blind, do not be so mad.
Acknowledge and admit here and now that it is your nature
that is wrong, your heart, your essential personality and
being. See further that as the years tend to pass, you do
not improve but tend to get worse. Has anyone ever
succeeded in turning his own hatred of God into love? He
may have given up this sin and that, but has he come to
love God? Has anyone ever done so? Can a man entirely
and completely change his own nature? Do you now love
God? for if you do not, you hate Him! No! no one has
ever succeeded in bringing this change about and yet it
has happened. Paul and millions of others at one time hated
Christ and persecuted His church, but afterwards came
to say, 'For me to live is Christ'. What had happened? Oh,
well, they had seen themselves as they really were in the
light of Christ, they cried out to Him for mercy. And they
obtained it, and a new nature also in addition. There it
is. If you do not recognize it you are damned. But, see
it and accept it, and you are safe to all eternity. Amen. [13]

In another sermon he pointed to the essence of the gospel in the following way:

> The salvation which we are offered in the gospel, far from being the result of man's efforts and endeavours, far from being a human and an earthly product is essentially divine and supernatural.[14]

Another recurring subject in the sermons of this period is the fight of faith. In a consideration of the great supper in Luke 14:16−24, he says:

> Something within them told them to go to the feast, to the supper, but the other something urged them to stay away. Where there is no conflict or struggle there is no life. Paul describes the sinner as being *dead* in trespasses and sins − lifeless. There is no real struggle in his life, no real fight. But of the Christian he says, 'the flesh lusteth against the Spirit, and the Spirit against the flesh, and these are contrary the one to the other'. As soon as the life of the Spirit, the life of Christ, enters our being there is inevitable conflict and struggle. The two eternally opposed forces are set against each other. Are you conscious of this? Is there a real struggle going on within you because of the claim of God and the claim of the devil? Are you at all disturbed? You say you desire to go to heaven, but have you realized that one only gets there as the result of the *fight* of faith? Turn to the New Testament again and read it carefully. Its picture of the Christian everywhere is of one who is fighting a great battle, with Jesus Christ as his leader and as his captain. He is out in a great crusade, a great war against sin and all iniquity. Are you in the fight, in the conflict? Christ calls upon all His true followers to enter the fray.[15]

This same emphasis occurs repeatedly in his preaching at Westminster Chapel, most notably in his series on Ephesians.

Amazing conversions

A second feature of those far-away days was the number of truly amazing conversions which took place. For substantive proof of this, we can again appeal to Mrs. Lloyd-Jones's record of the years 1927—38. She mentions the particularly glorious conversion of Georgie Sullivan, a bright lad of fifteen, who was suddenly taken seriously ill with a violent form of T.B. of the lungs. 'The Doctor' was about to leave a meeting at the chapel one night when he received a message that Georgie desperately wanted to see him. This is what happened next:

He went and found the boy in bed, with the typical hectic flush and shining eyes. He was very breathless but, 'Doctor, please tell me what it is all about? I sit and listen to you and I know it is right, but I don't understand, I don't know what I have to do.'

Martyn told him again, simply and plainly the way of salvation — was he sorry for all the things he had done which were displeasing to God? he must tell God so and ask him to forgive him, and God would do so because the Lord Jesus Christ had paid the penalty for them on the Cross. They would be blotted out for ever, and he would be able to stand before God and know that he was forgiven and received to Glory.

Georgie looked in wonderment as he said, 'Doctor, is that really the whole gospel?' and Georgie's eyes were opened in time. He died that night, and died with a heart at perfect peace and full of joy. Fifteen or under, eighty or over, and any age and every age in between. Age is not a barrier.[16]

No less remarkable were the conversions of Mark McCann, a brutal man with an uncontrollable temper[17], and Staffordshire Bill[18] (William Thomas was his real name), formerly a blaspheming drunkard but who, as a result of turning to God, became restrained and dignified, and whose death was both triumphant and tranquil. Events like these are thrilling fifty years on.

An expanding influence

A third important feature of his time in Aberavon was his increasing influence in Wales, in England, and eventually in America, which he first visited in 1932. In his biography Murray lists almost sixty places MLl-J visited in his first year at Sandfields.[19] In general, he would use the afternoons of Tuesday and Thursday for visits to other parts of Wales, both North and South, where his congregations were often huge. For example, at the 1935 South Wales Presbytery meeting at Llangeitho, he preached to a crowd of about 7,000 people. Obviously a crowd of this magnitude was rare, though in 1936 about 2,000 people attended one of his meetings in Felinfoel, West Wales.

During this time, too, he became increasingly well-known in England. One reason for this was his involvement with the student movement, the Inter-Varsity Fellowship[20] (now U.C.C.F.). Another reason was the fact that he received regular invitations to speak on English platforms and pulpits. One such engagement, on 3 December 1935 in a packed Albert Hall, had long-term consequences, because listening to him that night was Dr. Campbell Morgan. He immediately invited MLl-J to preach at Westminster Chapel that same month. So, on 29 December, he looked out from the pulpit at a building he had first entered twenty years previously. In the evening he spoke about 'The Narrowness of the Gospel', basing his remarks on Matthew 7:13-14 ('Enter ye in at the strait gate: for wide is the gate, and broad is the way, that leadeth to destruction . . .'). This sermon had been preached originally at Aberavon — in printed form it is now Sermon 20 in *Evangelistic Sermons at Aberavon*. In his opening comments he deals with the frequently heard claim that the average Christian is a narrow person:

> God forbid that we should ever really become narrow in the sense that the Pharisees were narrow, or that Judaism was narrow. God forbid that we should ever really reduce this glorious gospel of liberty to a mere number of prohibitions and restraints. But that is not our danger at all.

Our danger is that in our fear of being thought narrow, we should so swing over to the opposite extreme as eventually to become quite nondescript.[21]

Then in the body of his sermon he observes that the gospel message is narrow, in that it concerns itself with only one question: the human soul and its relationship with God:

We hear a good deal nowadays about the simple gospel. The secret of the simplicity of the gospel is this. Jesus of Nazareth, being the Son of God, and living in perfect correspondence and communion with His Father, had all knowledge. He knew what was important, and what was unimportant: and He ignored the unimportant, and gave Himself solely and entirely to the important things of life. He disregarded the irrelevant, and gave Himself utterly and only to the relevant, and to that which ultimately matters. The secret of the simplicity of the gospel lies in the fact that He brushed aside everything but the one supreme question of the soul's need. That is, clearly, an utter contradiction of all our modern ideas and conceptions.[22]

Secondly with the soul of the individual. He illustrates this by reference to the Samaritan woman (in John 4), then comments:

Yes, the gospel is a personal thing. We cannot be saved in families: we cannot be saved as a congregation. We cannot be saved collectively because we are all doing a certain amount of philanthropic work. We are saved one by one. It is a question of you and God.[23]

Thirdly the gospel affects our conduct and behaviour, negatively with regard to the teaching of the Ten Commandments, positively with reference to the Sermon on the Mount.

Finally he pin-points the gospel's declaration that salvation is possible only in and through one particular person (Jesus) and especially in his death. He makes this challenge to his congregation:

> If you can find liberation from your besetting sin without the power of the cross of Christ, carry on. If you can find peace and rest to your troubled conscience without believing in the death of the Son of God for you and for your sins; go ahead. If you can lie on your deathbed and think of facing a holy God without fear and without alarm, I really have nothing to say to you. But, if ever you should feel lost and miserable and wretched; if ever you should feel that all your righteousness is but as filthy rags; if ever you are filled with terror and alarm as you think of God, and His holy Law; if ever you feel utterly helpless and hopeless, then turn back to Him, the Christ of the cross, with His arms outstretched, who still says: 'Look unto me and be saved, all ye ends of the earth.' It is there that the whole of humanity is focused. He is the representative of the whole of mankind. He died for all.[24]

He concludes with a further challenge which is also an invitation to his hearers:

> If you accept the gospel and yield yourself to it, it will mean another birth for you; it will mean trial and temptation, it will mean persecution, it will mean the crucifixion and death of an 'old man' that is in you. BUT, it will lead to life which is life indeed, life more abundant, yea, the very life of God Himself.[25]

It was an invitation he was to extend to countless congregations for another forty-five years, with equal clarity, passion and utter conviction.

This sermon was significant in a number of different ways. According to Murray it was probably the first occasion he had preached in England on a Sunday to a non-Welsh Calvinistic Methodist congregation. It it too are clearly discernible Pauline elements: the insistence on the gospel as the *only* solution for

lost humanity; the essential link between that gospel and the way
in which a person behaves; the need for both negative and
positive in matters of faith and belief; and the assurance and
unshakeable confidence that belief and surrender to the gospel
brings.

A pastoral role

A fourth feature was the fact that he was the minister of a
church within a prescribed and easily identifiable community.
He had a role in that community which was not confined to the
church itself. He was frequently asked for advice on general
and medical matters. The 1930s in South Wales were grim years,
with the spectre of unemployment haunting many of its people.
Consequently, it was not surprising that the Labour Party (and
to a much lesser extent the Communist Party) should have made
much progress among people looking for an escape from poverty,
for a better world, and for a remedy for long-established social
ills. This was a black period of British industrial history in
general, with South Wales the blackest part of the whole country.

It is worth recalling, for example, that Edward VIII made a
much-heralded visit to these industrial heartlands in November
1936, and the empty shops, abandoned works, slag heaps, and
shabbily-clothed men in their hundreds caused him to utter the
now famous words to the men of Pontypool: 'You may be sure
that all I can do for you I will; we certainly want better times
brought to your valley.' Later while at Blaenavon he said:
'Something will be done about unemployment.' At Dowlais, he
looked at a large crowd of unemployed men and said, 'Something
must be done to find them work' — words which survive to this
day in the folk-lore of South Wales. Three weeks later he was
to abdicate, and South Wales remained a derelict area for a long
time to come.

MLl-J did not deal directly however with the prevailing
political situation, quite simply because he did not consider
politics to be part of the work he had been called to do. He
offered a vastly different form of Utopianism from that peddled
by J. Ramsay Macdonald (who at the 1922 General Election

easily won Aberavon for Labour) and Aneurin Bevan, the fiery
Welsh orator. It was not that he regarded political questions as
unimportant, but that such matters were not part of the church's
work. To him, as we well know from a reading of *Preaching
and Preachers*, the primary work of the church was the preaching
and interpreting of the Word of God. He believed that in all
aspects of life a Christian should think in a spiritual way, which
can only be achieved by a thorough knowledge and understanding
of the Scriptures. As he said in his sermon on 'The Strait Gate':

> If we are really serious about this matter of salvation, and
> not simply out to be clever, our business is not to express
> our own opinions and thoughts but to discover the mind
> of God. That alone can be found in the Bible.[26]

In another direction too, his whole outlook was different from
the devotees of a political creed. They loved to debate, to discuss,
to make ingenious debating points; whereas he was intent upon
declaring not a theory but an authoritative and inspired message,
in a spirit of 'reverence and godly fear'. His whole emphasis
therefore was far removed from the Socialism which gained such
a grip on the poverty-stricken valleys of South Wales in the 1930s.
In his view, Paradise could be regained; but not the Paradise
proposed by educationalists, philosophers, politicians, moralists,
or scientists. It was of course a spiritual paradise, which he
defined as follows in a sermon at Heath Evangelical (formerly
Presbyterian) Church, Cardiff, in 1978:

> This is the message of the Bible. You and I can enter into
> a spiritual Paradise *now*, at this very moment. Every
> Christian, every man who truly believes this message can
> enter into Paradise, spiritually, at this moment. What do
> you mean? you ask. Well, what I mean is this. What is
> Paradise? I say the most essential thing about Paradise is
> fellowship and communion with God. 'Being justified by
> faith we have peace with God through our Lord Jesus
> Christ.' 'God was in Christ reconciling the world unto
> Himself.' Any man who believes that is in Paradise. He

is reconciled to God, he has peace with God, he can pray
to God as Father, he can have communion with God as
Adam and Eve used to do freely before the Fall. He is
in the spiritual Paradise. Not only that. 'Being justified
by faith, we have peace with God through our Lord Jesus
Christ: by whom also we have access by faith.' We pray
to Him, He is our Father. We take our troubles and our
problems to Him, and He is with us, and we rejoice in
hope of the glory of God. You receive a new nature, and
the new nature does not love the darkness and hate the
light. It loves the light and it hates the darkness. We are
new men and women. We are made partakers of the divine
nature.[27]

Ironically, it has been suggested that MLl-J's preaching was
one factor in preventing Communism taking hold in South Wales
in the dark days of industrial depression, though I have not
discovered what his response to that opinion was.

For over eleven years MLl-J went determinedly and consistently on with the task of preaching the gospel in South Wales,
both in his own church and outside it. He did so before large
and small congregations and also in the open air, although this
latter practice ceased in 1938. At this time he began to feel, with
the same sort of piercing clarity that characterized his transition
from medicine to preaching, that his time at Sandfields was
drawing to its close. An added consideration was his extreme
tiredness after such a lengthy period of sustained preaching and
travelling. Clearly some sort of break was needed.

It is extremely interesting to observe the sequence of events
that followed. His decision to resign from the pastorate of
Sandfields was communicated to the church on Sunday 1 May
1938, and that same weekend he received a letter from Dr.
Campbell Morgan inviting him to share the pulpit of Westminster
Chapel with him for a period of six months. He found this
temporary arrangement acceptable, and towards the end of July
1938 the final packing was carried out in Victoria Terrace. Not
for fifteen years would he preach again at Sandfields, which
suggests that not only did he have a high regard for the church

and the people there, but also that the parting was not easy for him or indeed his family. Mrs. Lloyd-Jones has said as much, at the end of her book on those years in Aberavon:

> Leaving Sandfields was certainly not easy.
>
> At the time we sensed that we were being led step by step. We did not see everything clearly, but were walking by faith. As I look back now, over the passage of the years, the guidance of God seems as clear and inevitable as a route on a map, and I marvel afresh at the way all things worked together.[28]

They had been extremely happy years, when firm friendships were forged, important lessons were learned, and when they were conscious of God's guidance in a significant and valuable way. Again Mrs. Lloyd-Jones's words are relevant:

> We certainly could not have realised that we were moving from eleven-and-a-half years with our church family at Sandfields to spend thirty years with our much larger church family at Westminster Chapel! In a wonderful way, our time with the first family proved to be a preparation for serving in the new family, with which Martyn's name was more usually associated.[29]

What happened after that initial agreement with Dr. Campbell Morgan has been thoroughly and captivatingly recounted by Iain Murray. There is no need to repeat those facts again, except to note that by Sunday 23 April 1939, MLl-J had received and accepted a permanent call to Westminster Chapel as 'associate minister' with Dr. Campbell Morgan, an arrangement which was fruitful and harmonious for both of them − and this in spite of certain radical differences between the two men in approach and theology.

WAR

1939 was, of course, a catastrophic year for the whole world:

from its outset — indeed from the Munich crisis in September 1938 — most politicians and commentators were agreed on the inevitability of a Second World War. Its commencement, on 3 September, had two immediate effects. The first was that MLl-J's Induction to the co-pastorate of Westminster Chapel had to be cancelled, a fact which in and of itself did not cause him the slightest qualm or concern.

Dr. John Hutton had prepared an address intended for the Induction Service, which was subsequently published in *The British Weekly* (7 September 1939). In it he referred to God's sustaining help in his own ministry; stressed the need for the minister's vocation and work to be guided by the Pauline principle of 'Whatsoever things are true, whatsoever things are honourable, whatsoever things are just, whatsoever things are pure, whatsoever things are lovely, whatsoever things are of good report, if there be any virtue or praiseworthiness — keep thinking on these things'; stated his belief that 'We should never wish *Faith* to be anything but a fight. It is a good fight. It is the only good fight'; congratulated 'the Doctor' on coming to Westminster Chapel at the zenith of his 'natural powers'; and then concluded, by addressing him in the following manner:

> You come at a time when the world needs thinking, responsible men, humble and diffident, indeed, in view of their own poor wisdom and the present hazardousness, but strong and confident, knowing Him in Whom they have believed. We who know the Bible and accept it, are prepared for anything — seasons in the house of bondage with a crossing of the Red Sea; captivities which suffering souls turned into music which we still sing; a Cry of the Son of Man from the Cross of Calvary, when for one awful moment of His agony, feeling for the Hand of God, He missed it or was not aware that He held it; a cry which closed in a quiet prayer as of a tired child on the verge of sleep.
>
> We, whose souls rest amongst such things as on the breast of God, are prepared for anything. That is well, if with all that and as God's meaning for us in all that we

in such days refuse to be left out of the present battle of the Lord, which in the individual, in human societies, among governments and peoples, in the region of ideas and ideologies, with movements which barely skirt the edge of Anti-Christ the battle which is now raging. We are called not to be *spectators,* or *salt without the savour of salt*: of which sort of ineffectual misrepresentations of Himself our Lord declared that the contemporary world did well to despise them!

The second effect of the outbreak of war was that the Lloyd-Jones family moved to Haslemere, Surrey, where they remained for four years (1939–43).

During this period the regular services at Westminster Chapel carried on — with the exception of a brief period in the Livingstone Hall — until the explosion of a flying bomb nearly covered the preacher and congregation with a thin white dust, which at least one member assumed was the arrival of heaven. After this the services were again held in the Livingstone Hall, by which time (1944-5) the Lloyd-Jones family had settled in a manse in Ealing, West London. In the meantime MLl-J had also become sole pastor at Westminster Chapel, and he remained so until his retirement in 1968.

WESTMINSTER CHAPEL

So the best years of MLl-J's life were devoted to one of the largest Nonconformist congregations in London, the influence of which stretched beyond the confines of that huge city. To countless numbers in London, in the post-war period especially, the Sunday services were the pinnacles of the week. Many people travelled from afar to hear MLl-J preach. One Sunday in 1966 I attended Westminster Chapel and sat next to a family who said that they regularly drove up from Brighton; and, further, that they considered Westminster Chapel to be their 'home' church. In so doing they would have passed scores of other churches, so they must have got something special from the ministry there.

At Westminster, in an atmosphere of dignified and reverent worship, they were given a profound sense of a holy, divine, loving God who gave his son to redeem them from their sins and to himself, and also a full realization of their responsibility and obligation, in the light of the gospel, to live holy lives.

Such preaching has been described by a professional journalist:

> He likes to start slowly, with voice low, invariably he cruises round the runway several times before taking off. Sometimes you think you are encompassing Jericho with seven circuits. Imperceptibly, however, the message begins to grip and soon you are basking in the radiant sunshine of the Word preached with prophetic fire and unction. The theme so carefully laid out at the beginning reaches its climax and conclusion. The trumpets sound. The walls collapse. The citadel of the soul lies open to the conquest of truth. Once in full flight he is so vibrant spiritually and reaches such peaks of eloquence that even if you couldn't hear a word he said you would be impressed by the creative force of his gestures.[30]

The chapel would be crowded with people longing for know-ledge of the Word of God. Others were there because they had a special problem — be it personal, theological, psychological — and they were never disappointed, either with MLl-J's preaching or with his counsel and advice. There was one famous occasion in 1952 when fog, soot and smoke had combined to make it impossible for the vast majority of people to get to the evening service. The pews were deserted and an eerie atmosphere persisted outside, but he addressed the handful of people there with his usual passion and power, indeed as if the pews were bursting at the seams! Even in such dismal circumstances he attempted to bring his congregation into touch with the eternal and to fire their hearts with a sense of God's glory, compassion and grace.

No frills, then; no entertainment, no gimmicks, no topical illustrations, no anecdotes, but preaching which declared the 'manifold wisdom' of God in all its richness, vastness and incomparable grandeur; it dealt with the whole person in a way which affected people's lives. No attempt to be 'with it', or even to show why the gospel is 'relevant', or to deal with subjects of socio-political interest. Instead he presented the 'unsearchable riches of Christ'. There was no calling for 'decisions'. The very concept of people 'deciding' for Christ was, of course, an alien concept to MLl-J, who felt that such a policy often led to a superficial grasp of the wonder of salvation and of the heinousness of sin. Rather, he sought to lead men and women to the Lord Jesus Christ as the *only* remedy for helpless, poor, wretched sinners. No platitudes or fussy thinking, but rigorous, demanding preaching which sifted its hearers, with all the convicting power of the Holy Spirit.

It would not be appropriate here to cite the numerous examples of those who were converted or rededicated under his ministry (because the numbers were vast), but let him recount one remarkable example:

> I knew a poor man who had been converted from a terrible life of sin and who had become a fine Christian. That was when I was in South Wales. But, afterwards, unfortunately, for various reasons this poor fellow had become a backslider and had fallen very deeply into sin. He had run away from his wife and children to live with another woman of a very poor type. They had come to London and there they had lived in sin. He had squandered his money, and he had actually gone home and told his wife a lie in order to get further money out of her. The house in which they lived was in their joint names, but he got this changed and put into his name. Then he sold it in order to get the money. He had thus gone very very far into the 'far country', he had sinned terribly. But now the money had finished and the woman had deserted him. He was so utterly miserable and ashamed that he had solemnly decided to commit suicide, feeling that in his deep state of repentance God would forgive him. But he could not forgive himself, and he felt that he had no right ever to approach his family again. So he solemnly decided to walk to Westminster

Bridge and throw himself into the Thames. He was actually on the way to do this. Just as the poor soul arrived at the bridge, Big Ben struck half-past six — six-thirty. Suddenly a thought flashed into his mind and he said to himself, 'He (referring to me) will now be just entering his pulpit for his evening service.' So he decided that he would come and listen to me once more before he put an end to his life. He made his way to Westminster Chapel in about six minutes, got in through the front door, walked up the stairs and was just entering the gallery when he heard these words, 'God have mercy upon the backslider'. I uttered that petition in my prayer and they were literally the first words he heard. Everything was put right immediately, and he was not only restored but became an elder in a church in a suburb of London and rendered excellent service for a number of years.[31]

Equally numerous were the numbers of Christian people who were helped by his sermons, and MLl-J can tell the story himself:

Sometimes — and I am thinking especially of one particular occasion — I have gone out of the pulpit having only preached half my prepared sermon. I could not quite understand this on that particular occasion to which I am referring. But, however, it had happened, and so, in a sense, I was ready for the next Sunday morning. The next Sunday morning came and I preached the remainder of my original sermon, which had now become a sermon in and of itself. I found that I was given unusual liberty. A man came to me at the end and told me that there was a visitor there who would like to see me. He seemed to him to be a minister. Eventually I saw this minister whose home was thousands of miles away. He was so moved that he could scarcely speak. What had happened? Why was he so moved and affected? This man was quite certain that God had brought him there all that distance in order to hear that particular sermon. I have referred to this in the

Foreword of a little book called *Faith on Trial*; but it is worth repeating. I am sure that that man was right. But this is what astounded me. If I had not been dealt with on the previous Sunday in the way I have described, and restrained from preaching all my sermon, I would have preached on the previous Sunday what this man had just heard. But I had been restrained, I was only allowed to preach half my sermon the previous Sunday; the second half had been kept back. As I have said, I was a little disturbed about this but now it was perfectly clear to me. We do not control the situation; this is of God.[32]

MLl-J's routine at Westminster Chapel varied little in essential details from year to year. Apart from this two-month summer break, he preached three times each week, once on Friday evening and twice on Sundays. Often during the week he was away preaching in other parts of Britain, including of course Wales, where his engagements invariably consisted of two sessions: one in Welsh in the afternoon, and another in English in the evening. We have 'the Doctor's' own sanction[33] for saying that he tried to practise three types of preaching: evangelistic, which he felt ought to take place at least once a week; instructional of a primarily experimental nature, which he usually engaged in on Sunday mornings; and lastly a more purely instructional sort of preaching which he delivered on a weeknight.

RETIREMENT

He continued to discharge all his engagements as powerfully and as effectively as ever until the spring of 1968. On Friday 1 March 1968, he went on with his treatment of the Epistle to the Romans by concentrating on chapter 14:17: 'For the kingdom of God is not meat and drink; but righteousness, and peace, and joy in the Holy Ghost.' A sudden illness, however, requiring a serious operation in March, caused him to feel that — in God's will —

his ministry at Westminster Chapel ought to be drawn to a close. Consequently — and although he had made a very good recovery — he sent the following letter, dated Thursday 30 May 1968, to members at Westminster Chapel. It is printed here in full, because many readers will appreciate being able to see it:

I am sending you, individually, this letter which is really addressed to the entire church. My feelings as I do so are naturally mixed; and I assure you that nothing but the clearest possible conviction that I am obeying the unmistakable will of God would lead me to write in this way.

On one matter, however, my feelings are not mixed, and that is in profound gratitude to you all for your prayers on behalf of my wife and myself during these past three months. I was deeply conscious of being upheld and was able to enjoy 'the peace of God that passeth all understanding.'

The object of this letter is to inform you that last night in a Deacons' meeting, I gave the Deacons 3 months' notice of my retirement from the pastorate at Westminster Chapel. In other words I shall not be resuming my ministry amongst you as intended next September.

I thank God that this decision is not based on considerations of health. My medical advisers assure me that I can regard myself as having had 'a complete surgical cure,' and I am thankful to say that I am conscious of returning and increasing strength daily, and am already looking forward to fulfilling my various preaching engagements in various parts of the country, as from the first week in September. In other words, I am simply retiring from the pastoral charge of Westminster Chapel and hope to continue with all my other interests and activities.

My illness has simply acted as a precipitating factor in what was becoming an increasing conviction that I should take this step. However, owing to the wonderful and affectionate bonds that have bound us together for so long, I simply could not bring myself to do it. The moment I realised that I had to undergo an operation, I felt that God was saying to me, 'This is the end of one ministry and the beginning of another.' I said that to my dear wife and colleague before the operation, and, ever since, this conviction has deepened and become more and more clear.

The considerations that had weighed with me were the following. I am already past the age at which most people retire today. I have completed 30 unbroken years in the ministry of Westminster and given the best years of my life to it. This has meant that I have refused invitations from various parts of the world to lecture at colleges and seminaries and to address conferences of ministers, etc., etc. But, and perhaps most important of all, it has meant that I have only been able to publish but little of what I have preached at Westminster. Great pressure has been brought to bear on me to publish more, and recently, increasing pressure to write some account of my spiritual pilgrimage and what it was that led me − over 41 years ago − to leave the medical profession and become a whole time preacher of 'the glorious gospel of the blessed God.'

It is because I am as certain that God has now called me to fulfil these tasks, as I was of His call 41 years ago, that I am taking this step and informing you of it.

As I said at the beginning, my feelings are mixed, inevitably so, and I cannot imagine what my life will be like without preaching three times each week at Westminster Chapel − apart from my summer vacation. But when God calls, He is to be obeyed in spite of all natural feelings.

I know that you dear people will understand. If you do not, then my ministry has been in vain. I must not begin to write about the past and of the blessed and happy times that by the grace of God we have been allowed to have together. I cannot imagine a happier ministerial lot than mine has been. No minister could wish to have a more faithful and loyal people. I shall ever thank God for you all and those who have 'gone before'.

What things we have experienced! To a preacher nothing

is so wonderful as to feel the unction of the Holy Spirit
while preaching, and to hear of souls being brought under
conviction of sin, and then experiencing the new birth.
Thank God, that has often been our experience. But not
only that, one remembers marriages, births, deaths, even
war and bombing, reconstruction of buildings and many
other matters faced together; but above all I shall treasure
the privilege of ministering to those with grievous
problems of various types and enjoying the trust and
confidence of those passing through dark and deep waters.

But I must refrain. I know that you will all stand together
and commit the future of our beloved church to God. It
is His, not ours; and as He has led, He will continue to
lead. As I have often reminded you, what happens at
Westminster Chapel is observed and scrutinised far and
wide, imitated and criticised. Your responsibility therefore
is a very great one but I am confident that, as always in
the past, you will face it, shoulder it, and rise to it in a
manner that will bring great glory and honour to our
blessed Lord and Saviour.

I need not assure you of my constant prayers and
thoughts, and what applies to you will also apply to your
new minister and leader.

Thus, with loving and most tender greetings from my
wife and myself — what I and my ministry owe to her you
all know — I subscribe myself for the last time.

Your privileged and unworthy minister and friend,

D. M. LLOYD-JONES.

This letter is an important historical document for an
understanding of his life and career, mirroring as it does his
complete dependence on God, his obvious delight in everything
that God has been able to achieve through him at Westminster,
his wish to bring his sermons — in response to many requests
— to a wider audience, his debt to his wife for all her sustaining
help, and his emphasis on the life of prayer.

MLl-J had a lengthy retirement: thirteen years. During those
years his life differed little in essence from that which he had

pursued in the ministry for over forty years. He continued to
live in London and went on with his preaching and teaching
ministry, as well as giving advice on personal and pastoral
matters. But more importantly, he was able to prepare for
publication two of the series of sermons he had preached on
Romans and Ephesians. They were published as follows:*

1970: *Romans 3:20-4:25: Atonement and Justification*
1971: *Romans 5: Assurance*
1972: *Romans 6: The New Man*
       Ephesians 2: God's Way of Reconciliation
1973: *Romans 7:1-8:4: The Law: Its Functions and Limits*
1974: *Romans 8:5-17: The Sons of God*
       Ephesians 5:18-6:9: Life in the Spirit
1975: *Romans 8:17-39: The Final Perseverance of the Saints*
1976: *Ephesians 6:10-13: The Christian Warfare*
1977: *Ephesians 6:10-20: The Christian Soldier*
1978: *Ephesians 1:1-23: God's Ultimate Purpose*
1979: *Ephesians 3:1-21: The Unsearchable Riches of Christ*
1980: *Ephesians 4:1-6: Christian Unity*

In addition, in 1971 he published the lectures he had given
at Westminster Theological Seminary in the spring of 1969, under
the title of *Preacher and Preachers*. Since his death the following
volumes have been published:

1982: *Ephesians 4:17-5:17: Darkness and Light*
1983: *Expository Sermons on 2 Peter*
1983: *Evangelistic Sermons at Aberavon*
1984: *Joy Unspeakable: The Baptism with the Holy Spirit*
1985: *Prove All Things: The Sovereign Work of the*
       Holy Spirit
1985: *Romans 1: The Gospel of God*
1986: *The Cross: God's Way of Salvation*

* The order of title and sub-title has been reversed, where appropriate,
to show clearly which biblical passages are expounded.

These volumes are almost verbatim versions of the original sermons. As such, there is no attempt in them at literary polish or sophistication. That they were printed in full was due to MLl-J's strongly held conviction that preparing sermons for a reading public rather than a listening one leads to their being 'something quite nondescript'. Inevitably this means the appearance in his printed works of certain colloquialisms, repetitions, and the frequent use of rhetorical questions which would probably have been edited out for a primarily reading audience. They are sermonic in flavour and form, and the living voice is present in them to a remarkable degree.

These volumes have proved to be extraordinarily popular, and the reasons are not difficult to identify. The oratory and eloquence of the living voice shines through them. They blend theological understanding with a warm-hearted pastoral intent; and they analyse in detail some of the great and timeless truths of the Bible. They also have a spiritual common sense which is often lacking in many evangelical preachers. And finally, they are unequivocal and firm.

The regular pattern of preaching, advising others and editorial work went on unabated until 1979 when, struck again by illness, MLl-J was forced to cancel all his engagements, though by the Spring of 1980 he again took up some of his preaching appointments. On Wednesday 4 June 1980, for example, he preached at Ashford Congregational Church, Middlesex. He took as his theme 'The Nature of the Christian Ministry', basing his remarks on 2 Corinthians 4:5: 'For we preach not ourselves, but Christ Jesus the Lord; and ourselves your servants for Jesus' sake.' His final sermon was preached at Barcombe Baptist Chapel on 8 June 1980, at the opening of that chapel, when he spoke on Joshua 4:6, 'What mean ye by these stones?'. His last sermon in Welsh had been delivered on 14 May 1980 at Aberystwyth.

From then on, however, his medical condition deteriorated and he had to face wearisome treatment at Charing Cross Hospital — which, according to Sir Fred Catherwood, 'he faced, with courage and dignity'.[34] He was able however to continue working on his manuscripts and also to advise other ministers.

By Christmas 1980 he was too unwell to carry on with these tasks, though he co-operated fully with his biographer, Iain Murray, who has said that MLl-J's involvement 'continued almost until his death on March 1, 1981'.[35]

News of his death spread rapidly throughout the Principality. For many, tears seemed natural and inevitable, not least because a courageous, wise and consistent counsellor had been taken from the battle. Many felt, in Hugh Morgan's words, 'bereft and unsafe'.[36]

TRIBUTES

'The Doctor' was buried on the afternoon of Friday, 6 March 1981, at Bethel Calvinistic Methodist Chapel in the small market town of Newcastle Emlyn, about ten miles from the old town of Cardigan. The number attending the funeral has been variously reckoned, but a conservative estimate would be at least 1,000, itself an indication of the esteem and love so many had for him.

The service, conducted by the Revd. Vernon Higham of Cardiff, had three main elements: Welshness, assurance, and triumph. It commenced with the singing of the Welsh hymn, *Cyfamod hedd, cyfamod cadarn Duw*, which may be translated into English as, 'Covenant of peace, steadfast (or strong) covenant of God'. The Revd. Elwyn Davies, Secretary of the Evangelical Movement of Wales, read 1 Corinthians 15:35-58, with its resonant message that death *will* ultimately and finally be defeated and that 'this mortal must must put on immortality'. Following the Revd. Hywel Jones's prayer, the congregation sang 'The God of Abraham Praise'. Then Vernon Higham preached on the text, 'For so an entrance shall be ministered unto you abundantly into the everlasting kingdom of our Lord and Saviour Jesus Christ.' This verse was all the more poignant for Higham, because the last time he saw MLl-J he had requested him to pray for an abundant entry into glory. Students of his life and ministry will doubtless recall his sermon on 'Life and Death' which was the fifth of twenty-five sermons he preached on 2 Peter between

October 1946 and March 1947. In it he says that one of the
supreme tests of the Christian profession 'is the way in which
we face old age, is the way in which we face death'.[37] Later in
the same sermon he said:

> The Christian when he dies, does not cross the bar and
> set out to sea. No; it is rather, as Charles Wesley put it:
>
> > *Safe into the haven guide,*
> > *O receive my soul at last*
>
> — that is the Christian view of death. It is going home,
> it is entering into harbour, 'An entrance will be ministered
> unto you'. Not a setting out on to an uncharted ocean, not
> going vaguely into some dim, unchartered world. Not at
> all, but an entrance into the haven, going home. What does
> it all mean? It means that the Christian dies like that
> because he knows God. He has striven diligently to know
> Him better and better. He knows Christ. He knows where
> he is going. He does not feel lonely as he is dying, because
> Christ is with him. He has promised, 'I will never leave
> thee, nor forsake thee'.[38]

He concluded,

> But above all, as the Christian is entering the harbour a
> voice says, 'Come, ye blessed of my Father, inherit the
> kingdom prepared for you from the foundation of the world
> — enter the joy of your Lord.' That is how the Christian
> dies. Don't you feel, as you hear that, that you want to
> say with one of old, 'Let me die the death of the righteous
> and let my last end be like his'? Well, there is but one way
> which guarantees the abundant entrance in the everlasting
> Kingdom. It is this: 'Blessed are they that do his
> commandments, that they may have right to the tree of
> life, and may enter in through the gates into the city.'[39]

The same note of assurance and certainty was evident in

Higham's message on the simplicity and power of the gospel, to which he gave the following headings: the mystery of the faith, the mastery of death, and the majesty of heaven. A second Welsh hymn, *Mae ffrydiau 'ngorfoledd yn tarddu/ O ddisglair orseddfainc y ne'* ('A torrent of rejoicing, proceeding from the splendour of heaven's throne'). After this the Revd. Graham Harrison of Newport led in prayer and pronounced the benediction. The service of committal at the graveside was conducted by the Revd. Omri Jenkins, of the European Missionary Fellowship.

The obituaries and notices appearing after his death stressed different aspects of the character and achievements of 'The Doctor'. Part of the *Daily Telegraph's* tribute to him said this:

> Possessed of the Welsh gifts of speech and presentation of the spoken word, Martin (sic) Lloyd-Jones added to them his scientific approach which gave him a persuasive, argumentative manner in the pulpit. He relied little on oratory as such, but always moved his audience by reasoned statement. He was especially gifted in expository preaching, and for one not trained in theology, his grasp of biblical fundamentals was remarkable.[40]

The Times hailed MLl-J as 'the last of a long line of great Welsh preachers', commenting: 'His exact medical training disciplined his thinking and teaching and helped him to deal with those pastoral problems on the frontier between the physical and the spiritual.' It also declared that 'he had the rare combination of compelling logic and vivid enlightenment and was in the tradition of Calvinistic Methodists, combining clear doctrine with warm personal application,' and said: 'He was a respected and well-loved Christian leader who will be greatly missed' — a sentiment with which few would disagree.

To Terry Campbell in the *Western Mail*, MLl-J was quite simply 'unique'. He added this opinion: 'He was undoubtedly the finest pulpit orator of his generation and was the last of the great preachers in the true evangelical tradition. He was an outstanding leader of British Nonconformity.' The same writer referred to MLl-J's dislike of gimmicks and manipulation of the emotions, his integrity, his love of children, and the secure base of his happy family life. A warmth is apparent in this tribute to 'A king of orators', which ends with this statement: 'His power lay not in his eloquence: his secret was his faith and his rectitude. It was really as simple as that.'

In the opinion of D. Hughes Jones in the Welsh publication, *Y Faner*, 'the Doctor' was in every sense of the word 'big': 'He was big as a preacher and as a man. In him Protestantism had a 'Pope' who gave his blessing on everything he considered to be fitting of the gospel and who gave his judgement on everything opposed to it' (my translation). The same writer also makes reference to MLl-J's fundamental and biblical viewpoint on all matters of faith, and his robust and steadfast refusal to water-down the gospel in order to make it 'attractive'.

The Welsh Presbyterian Church's weekly newspaper, *Y Goleuad*, described him as one of Wales's most brilliant sons, and expressed the opinion that the secret of his appeal as a preacher lay in 'his deep convictions regarding the place of preaching in the life of the church', adding: 'He believed passionately that preaching the gospel was the highest of all callings, and that the greatest need of the church was to hear the faithful preaching of God's Word' (my translations). This notice ended by regretting the closing of another chapter in the history of Welsh preaching, not least because nobody else is likely to draw the crowds in the way MLl-J did.

The *Bible-Presbyterian BANNER* obituary commented on his roles as 'Evangelist, Pastor, Author, Christian Leader', stating: 'To all Christians, he was one who, both in the pulpit and print, expounded the Word of God with authority, simplicity and power.' In the same issue (May-June 1981), Dr. Tom Siang Hwa added a personal postscript:

> During my postgraduate sojourn in London in 1958-1959, I had the privilege of attending Westminster Chapel for seven months, to be blessed by the ministry of the Word from the 'Doctor,' as Martyn Lloyd-Jones was affectionately referred to. Together with my wife and daughter we

never missed a Sunday. The depth of his expository preaching, the incisiveness of his observations, the logic of his arguments and the clinical approach of his scientific mind made the Gospel simply profound, yet profoundly simple.

Other obituaries called attention to MLl-J's ability to fill some of the largest arenas in the country (for example, the old Free Trade Hall, Manchester and the Usher Hall in Edinburgh, and the Albert Hall in London), his independence of outlook, his appeal to the consciences of his hearers, his lack of airs and graces, his unshakeable belief in the authority of the Scriptures, and his logical and orderly mind.

Doubtless MLl-J would have objected to the portrayal of himself as a sort of heroic figure to countless thousands of people all over the world: but that is what he was, and that is what the various obituaries attempted to say, though for him it was sufficient to be able to say 'I determined not to know anything among you, save Jesus Christ and him crucified.' To him nothing else mattered, but I think it only right and fitting that his work and legacy should have been recorded in the written word — and thus made a matter of historical fact. It is not pretentiousness in my case to add those immortal words from Chaucer's *General Prologue:*

He was a very parfit gentil knyght.

A Thanksgiving Service was held at Westminster Chapel on Monday 6 April 1981, chaired by the Revd. John Caiger. Other speakers included Dr. R.T. Kendall (the present minister at Westminster Chapel); Professor G.N.M. Collins, of the Free Church College, Edinburgh, who spoke of MLl-J's profound influence on Scotland; Dr. Gaius Davies (from the world of medicine); Dr. Robin Wells (General Secretary of the U.C.C.F., formerly the I.V.F.); the Revd. Iain Murray, who spoke about his printed works; Mr. M.J. Micklewright, a senior deacon at Westminster Chapel; the Revd. Omri Jenkins, who spoke of MLl-J as a preacher; and finally the Revd. Peter Lewis, of

Nottingham, who preached on Revelation 17-18.

The Thanksgiving Service was a blend of past and future. There was deep and abiding gratitude for all that MLl-J had meant for innumerable people and for all he had achieved as a preacher, pastor, counsellor, friend and author. There was confidence in the continuing grace of God for the future raising up of preachers, who like him, would feel that there is 'nothing in life to be compared with the preaching of this glorious and incomparable gospel',[41] and who would always remember that 'the business of preaching is not to entertain but to lead people to salvation, to teach them how to find God'.[42]

Finally, at the particular request of the Lloyd-Jones family, the Revd. John Caiger read John Bunyan's account of the summons of Mr. Valiant for Truth:

> After this it was noised abroad that Mr. Valiant for Truth was taken with a summons and had this for a token that the summons was true that his pitcher was broken at the fountain. When he understood it, he called for his friends and told them of it. Then said he, "I am going to my Father's. And though with great difficulty I am got hither, yet now I do not repent me of all the trouble I have been at to arrive where I am. My sword I give to him that shall succeed me in my pilgrimage, and my courage and skill to him that can get it. My marks and scars I carry with me to be a witness for me that I have fought His battles who now will be my rewarder."
>
> When the day that he must go hence was come, many accompanied him to the riverside, into which, as he went, he said, "Death, where is thy sting?" And as he went down deeper, he said, "Grave, where is thy victory?" And so he passed over and all the trumpets sounded for him on the other side.

One can think of no more fitting epitaph for the life of MLl-J.

CHAPTER 3

The Significance of His Career

THE PREACHER

MLl-J's life was primarily devoted to preaching — not teaching or ministering, not pastoring or shepherding, but preaching, because that is what he was *par excellence*: a preacher. He was often referred to as the 'Prince of Preachers'. This was a task to which he was absolutely convinced God had called him, and at the beginning of *Preaching and Preachers* he said this: 'The work of preaching is the highest and the greatest and the most glorious calling to which anyone can ever be called.' (p.9) He went on to state his belief that 'the most urgent need in the Christian Church today is true preaching; and as it is the greatest and most urgent need in the Church it is obviously the greatest need of the world also.' (p.9)

The key phrase in this forthright statement is, of course, 'true preaching'. To him this was *expository preaching*, which he defines in his volume on *2 Peter* as 'preaching which is concerned to expound the Word of God and not merely to express the ideas of the preacher, preaching which is not merely topical and intended to suit the popular palate and conditions prevailing at the moment'.[1] In his preface to Volume One of *Studies in the Sermon on the Mount*, he says this:

> A sermon is not an essay and is not meant, primarily, for publication, but to be heard and to have an immediate impact upon the listeners. This implies, of necessity, that it will have certain characteristics which are not found and are not desirable in written studies. To prune it of these, if it should be subsequently published, seems to me to be quite wrong, for it then ceases to be a sermon and becomes something quite nondescript. I have a suspicion that what accounts for the dearth of preaching at the present time is the fact that the majority of printed books of sermons have clearly been prepared for a reading rather than a listening public. Their flavour and form are literary rather than sermonic.[2]

He had equally decisive views concerning the *form* of his sermons:

> These are expository sermons which apart from minor corrections and adjustments were delivered as printed here. They are not lectures nor a running commentary on verses or passages. They are expositions which take the form of a sermon.
>
> It has always been my view that this is how Scripture should be handled. Commentaries are of great value in arriving at an accurate understanding of the text, yet at their best they are only of value as scaffolding in the erection of a building. Moreover, it is vital that we should understand that an epistle such as this is only a summary of what the Apostle Paul preached. He explains that in chapter 1 verses 11-15. He wrote the Epistle because he was not able to visit them in Rome. Had he been with them he would not merely have given them what he says in this Letter, for this is but a synopsis. He would have preached an endless series of sermons as he did daily in the school of Tyrannus (Acts 19.9) and probably have often gone on

until midnight (Acts 20.7). The business of the preacher
and teacher is to open out and expand what is given here
by the Apostle in summary form.[3]

But perhaps the best—and crispest—definition he gave of
preaching is this sentence from *Preaching and Preachers*:
'Preaching is theology coming through a man who is on fire'.
He saw the chief end of preaching as giving men and women
'a sense of God and His presence'. He adds this personal
postscript:

> As I have said already, during this last year I have been
> ill, and so have had the opportunity, and the privilege, of
> listening to others, instead of preaching myself. As I have
> listened in physical weakness this is the thing I have looked
> for and longed for and desired. I can forgive a man for
> a bad sermon, I can forgive the preacher almost anything
> if he gives me a sense of God, if he gives me something
> for my soul, if he gives me the sense that, though he is
> inadequate himself, he is handling something which is very
> great and very glorious, if he gives me some dim glimpse
> of the majesty and the glory of God, the love of Christ
> my Saviour, and the magnificence of the Gospel. If he does
> that I am his debtor, and I am profoundly grateful to him.[4]

He frequently returned to the theme of 'true' preaching. Here
is another succinct comment: 'The true preacher does not seek
for truth in the pulpit; he is there because he has found it'.[5] It
all seems so simple, so obvious, so profound.

What then were the main characteristics of MLl-J's preaching?
Firstly, it was

Authoritative preaching

It was positive and certain, confident and assured. It had a rock-
like quality, utterly dogmatic and assertive. Alongside this quality
was its fearlessness, its declarative nature. It had a convincing
and convicting quality, and this authority was certainly an

important factor for the people who crowded Westminster Chapel
– and those before that in Wales – during his ministry there.
The congregations during his heyday were huge: about 1,500
on a Sunday morning, 2,000 on a Sunday evening.

The authority of his preaching may be directly traced to the
fact that he wanted the divine authority to be given the fullest
possible place in his sermons. So he was not concerned with
intruding himself into them. On the contrary, he wished God
to speak and to influence the minds, hearts and consciences of
his hearers. I shall never forget hearing him preach on 1
Corinthians 2:1-4 in Heath Presbyterian Church, Cardiff, and
marvelling at the boldness, the complete assurance that the
gospel brings of freedom from sin, the life of the Spirit, and
the certain hope of being with Christ. That night in Cardiff
people filled every seat in the Chapel and also occupied the
aisles, the window-sills and the gangways – in short, they were
crammed in to overflowing. There was the usual MLl-J opening:
his cultured Welsh voice quietly stating the abiding and sublime
truths of God's Word, the essential principles; then their
amplification, analysis, and application to the lives of believers.
There was the perfect combination of teaching concerning
doctrine and behaviour. The sermon as a whole was designed
to bring non-Christians to faith in Christ, and Christians to full
maturity in him. At a time of considerable personal doubt, this
sermon strengthened and encouraged me to go on with the 'fight
of faith'. The beauty of it was that it was all so cogently,
intelligently, and persuasively argued. Here was a man preaching
a message which God had revealed to him, the deep and
meaningful outpouring of a soul after a meeting with God. The
mind was informed, the heart warmed, and Jesus Christ extolled.
Hundreds of people went out that night more determined to battle
with the powers of darkness than when they entered the building.
It was preaching of the most anointed sort.

His authority was not only apparent when expounding the great
doctrines of the Christian faith, but also when defending it against
liberals and detractors. This apologetic element is implicit in
all true preaching, and MLl-J never shirked the duty of defending
the faith when it was attacked by the so-called 'Higher Critics',

or by those who wished to water down the Scriptures, or by those
who propounded wrong or unbalanced teaching. Here he is, for
example, dealing with the ideas of T.S. Eliot and Middleton
Murray:

'They advocate a religious society and a Christian
education — or what they call such — simply because they
have found all else to fail, and because they think that this
is more likely to be successful. But they fail to realize that
before you can have a Christian society and Christian
education you must first of all have Christians. No
education or culture, no mode of training, will ever
produce Christians and the corresponding morality. To do
that we must come face to face with God and see our sin
and helpless plight; we must know something about the
wrath of God, and repent before Him and then receive
His gracious offer of salvation in Jesus Christ His Son.
But that is not mentioned. Men ever desire the benefits
of Christianity without paying the price.'[6]

Of course this authoritative preaching gripped the minds of
his hearers, for as Sir Fred Catherwood explains:

His style was that of sharp clinical diagnosis, analysing
the worldly view, showing its futility in dealing with the
power and persistence of evil, and contrasting the Christian
view, its logic, its realism and its power. He had the ability
to clothe his clinical analysis with vivid and gripping
language, so that it stayed in the mind. He could be
scathing about the follies of the world and give a
contrasting vision of the wisdom and power of God in a
way which brought strong reaction from his audience.
People would walk out, determined never to come again;
yet, despite themselves, they would be back in the pew
the next Sunday until, no longer able to resist the message,
they became Christians.[7]

Biblical preaching

Never could it be said that his preaching depended upon frills or entertainment, gimmicks, 'up-to-date' illustrations, or 'relevant' discussion of the burning issues of the day; what he sought to declare was 'the whole counsel of God'. It was preaching soaked in the Word of God, and it dealt with the whole person. This last point is worth stressing, because although he did not major in contemporary events, his preaching had considerable impact. He saw — and consistently taught — that for salvation to be worthwhile it must affect and control a person's mind, reason, heart and emotions. It was, he held, something radically life-transforming. He wanted a person's response to the whole of life (not merely isolated parts of it) to be thoroughly Christian, thoroughly biblical. As a result he never peddled easy answers or soft options; such remedies never appealed to him and so he did not advocate them.

Needless to say, his view of the Bible was an exalted one. He conceived of it as the 'Word of God . . . the greatest Book, because it is a Divine Book'. Frequently in his sermons he would allude to the nature, the power, and the uniqueness of the Bible. To give but one example, consider this extract from 'Sound An Alarm', a sermon preached at a Civic Service in Cardiff on 1 January 1957:

> The Bible claims to be the Word of God — the Word of God about Himself, the Word of God about man, the Word of God about the world, the Word of God which tells us why the world is as it is, and the Word of God as to how the world can be put right. That is the whole case of the Bible. It claims that it has a unique teaching with respect to the problem of man. It tells us right at the very beginning that man's troubles in this world and in this life, whether you think of man as an individual or man as a collection of people, have come upon him because of something that happened at the very beginning, at the very dawn of history. The Bible says that man fell from God, that he sinned against God, and that as the result of so doing he

is in a state of sin. It says that man, the whole world, has been in that condition ever since the Fall, and that this is the most important and the most significant thing about man that we can ever learn and understand.

In view of this, the Bible says that the whole story of man from that first beginning has always been the same. It does not matter what changes there may be, the real truth is that man is in a state of sin and alienation from God, and that is the cause of all his troubles and of all his problems. So whenever you read your Bible, it does not matter whether you read the Old Testament or the New Testament, whether it is an historical portion, prophetic portion or Psalm, it does not matter whether you are reading about one man, or whether you are reading about the Christian of Israel as a nation, you will find that the story, the message, is always exactly the same in principle. It is always this story of man in trouble because he is sinful. That is why the Bible is always contemporary, and always up to date, for it says that man is still what man has always been ever since that original sin, ever since that first fall in the Garden of Eden.[8]

Equally frequently he would comment on the essence of the biblical method:

The Bible always gives us comfort and encouragement by means of doctrine — never apart from doctrine. Take that great eighth chapter of the Epistle to the Romans. It is one of the most theological, doctrinal passages to be found anywhere in the Bible; and yet there is nothing more comforting, more consoling and more encouraging. The argument is this: 'Whom he did predestinate, them he also called: and whom he called, them he also justified: and whom he justified, them he also glorified.' Doctrine! and apart from that doctrine, the Bible has no comfort and consolation to offer us.[9]

So he deliberately set out to allow the Bible to be its own

interpreter and arbitrator. To illustrate the extent to which the
Bible is quoted directly in his sermons, I counted the biblical
references in his second sermon on Romans 3:25, entitled 'The
Blood of Christ'. He refers directly and fully to the following
verses: Acts 20:28; Romans 5:9; Ephesians 2:13; Hebrews 9:12,
9:22, 10:19; 1 John 1:7; Romans 5:21; John 1:29; Matthew
5:17-18; Matthew 20:28; Luke 24:44-45; 1 Corinthians 5:7;
Revelation 1:5; John 3:16, and Romans 1:32. He also refers to
the following chapters: Isaiah 53, 1 Peter 2, and Romans 4.

It hardly needs pointing out that MLl-J's knowledge of the
Scriptures was encyclopedic. Throughout his life he read the
Bible systematically. He taught that the right way of approaching
it was carefully and studiously; to read it as a whole, with fairness
and an open mind, with a spirit of humility and with a willingness
to learn, and finally prayerfully. From the early days of his
ministry in Aberavon he made it his business to bring himself
under the authority of the Scriptures, prepared to be illumined
and illuminated by the Holy Spirit, in an attitude of obedience,
and with an unquenchable enthusiasm for its essential messages.
Commenting on the word 'therefore' (Ephesians 4:1), he says
this:

> 'Therefore' is a word which in a very practical way tells
> us how to read the Scriptures. We need to be taught how
> to read the Scriptures. The main principle is, as I have
> been indicating, that we must never pick and choose in
> our reading of the Scriptures. We must read all the
> Scriptures, every part of the Scripture. Instinctively we
> do not like to do so; we have our favourite passages; there
> are certain Psalms or portions in the New Testament
> Epistles, or certain pictures in the Gospels in which we
> delight, and which always move us when we read them.
> The tendency and the danger is to be ever going back to
> such portions. But that is the high road to the develop-
> ment of an unbalanced and lop-sided Christian life and
> experience. Our invariable rule with the Bible should be
> to read it from Genesis to Revelation, to read it constantly
> right through, not leaving out anything, but following it

through, and being led by it. If we believe that it is the Word of God, that all of it is the Word of God, it follows that there is a meaning and a significance in every part, in the historical portions and the genealogies as well as the explicitly teaching portions. So we must go through and read them all, and try to grasp the meaning of all.[10]

Thus his approach to any issue or problem was quite simply to start with the biblical viewpoint, with the fundamental doctrines and principles, rather than with the immediate situation. To argue from large principles was his perennial method — something which is apparent, for example, in his sermons on Psalm 73, later published as *Faith on Trial*. And from the vantage point of the biblical perspective he proceeded to show, time after time, how bankrupt, how devoid of any real or substantial comfort is the non-Christian view of life; and from this standpoint he was able to help, comfort, and sustain others. The sermons referred to above on Psalm 73 are a notable illustration of this:

The preparation and the preaching of the following sermons, expounding this rich teaching on successive Sunday mornings, was to me a labour of love and a true joy. The sermon entitled 'Nevertheless' in the series was used of God to bring immediate relief and great joy to a man who was in a great agony of soul and near breaking point. He had travelled some 6,000 miles and had reached London only the previous day. He was convinced, and still is, that God in His infinite grace had brought him that distance to hear that sermon.[11]

Analytical preaching

As a medical physician MLl-J had insisted on the value of a correct and perceptive diagnosis, and he brought to his preaching the same insistence on the absolute necessity of a searching analysis of the soul's need. To this end all his learning and all the resources of his heart and mind were brought to bear. His preaching had a pellucid clarity, as this extract from *Romans 3:20-4:25*, where he is laying down the essential argument of Romans chapter 4, shows:

> In verses 1 to 5 he takes the case of Abraham, giving the facts and the statements of the Scriptures on the facts. In verses 6, 7 and 8 we have what David said explicitly in Psalm 32. Then from verse 9 to verse 12 he points out that all this had happened to Abraham before he was circumcised; so circumcision cannot be the vital thing. Then in verses 13 to 17 he proves that this also was before the Law had been given. Indeed God had ordered things in this way in order that He might show once and for ever that salvation is by grace, through faith, not by circumcision or by the Law, because grace is the only way whereby it can be made certain and sure. From verse 18 to the end of the chapter he gives an exposition of how this faith was manifested in the case of Abraham and how it all redounds to the glory of God. At the end he brings it back to the point at which he originally started, by saying, As God did it then He is still doing it now: 'Now it was not written for his sake alone, that it was imputed to him; but for us also, to whom it shall be imputed, if we believe on him that raised up Jesus our Lord from the dead; who was delivered for our offences and raised again for our justification.'[12]

He then asks this revealing question: 'Are you not moved to admiration at the wonderful way in which this Apostle is able to deploy a great argument?'

Ultimately his aim was to lay bare God's truth and to stress that only truth can make a person really free. Such preaching of course annoyed some, outraged others, but liberated many more.

'The Doctor' always showed great pastoral concern for those who were suffering, as this sentence from his letter of 30 May 1968 to members of Westminster Chapel shows: 'Above all I shall treasure the privilege of ministering to those with grievous

problems of various types and enjoying the trust and confidence
of those passing through dark and deep waters.' But he opposed
any suggestion that the church should be a greenhouse for tender
plants. In *Evangelistic Sermons*, he points out that there are many
good reasons why a church should have an unsettling effect on
some of its members:

> The church is regarded as a sort of dispensary where drugs
> and soothing mixtures are distributed and in which
> everyone should be eased and comforted. And the one
> theme of the church must be 'the love of God.' Anyone
> who happens to break these rules and who produces a
> disturbing effect upon members of his congregation is
> regarded as an objectionable person, is disliked and is
> charged with voicing his own opinions and prejudices
> instead of preaching the gospel which is said to be nothing
> but a constant refrain concerning 'the love of God'. Now,
> as I have already indicated, that charge may be perfectly
> true, a man's ministry may be objectionable just because
> he is a mean, petty soul who makes the pulpit 'a coward's
> castle' and uses it simply that he may vent his spleen upon
> his own personal enemies. But that is not the only
> condition under which a ministry can make itself objec-
> tionable to certain people — there is another reason, and
> that the highest and best reason, namely that the man is
> simply and honestly preaching the gospel of Jesus
> Christ.[13]

This was the blend of intelligence and deeply spiritual thinking
that made him so valuable to the student body (formerly the
I.V.F., now U.C.C.F.), as we shall see later in this chapter. It
was also the blend which attracted thinking people in general
to his preaching: people of all shades of opinions (Methodists,
Baptists, Brethren, Church of England and others all found
spiritual sustenance and encouragement at Westminster Chapel).
This capacity for analytical thought is nowhere more apparent
than in *Christian Unity: An Exposition of Ephesians 4:1-16*, in
which he stresses time after time the need for correct thinking

on this vexed matter. Here is one of his initial comments on Paul's
method of dealing with church unity:

> He does not leave it as a personal appeal to us to be kind
> and longsuffering and good. These graces are essential
> but the fundamental principle is that we should see
> ourselves as members of the Church, and see the Church
> as a reflection on earth of the oneness of the Triune God
> — Three in One, One in Three, Holy Spirit, Son, Father.
> Surely it must be evident that the real trouble with modern
> Christians is that they neglect doctrine! We talk about being
> practical, but we cannot be practical unless we know how
> to be practical, and why we should be so. Before we can
> respond to direct personal appeals we have got to see what
> we are, where we are, and where God has placed us. We
> have been 'called'.[14]

His analytical skill was never more in evidence than when
dealing with the 'wiles of the devil' or with the teaching of the
'false prophets', and he very often returned to the idea of testing
the messages of such people in a diagnostic way, as this extract
shows:

> But, still more seriously, the ultimate way of testing a
> message is this. The false prophet and teacher denies the
> Lord that has bought him — 'denying the Lord that bought
> them' and there are more ways than one of doing this.
> Sometimes they deny the Lord that has bought them by
> just leaving Him out altogether. They purport to give a
> Christian message, and yet the name of Christ is never
> mentioned. God is mentioned, but Christ the Lord is not.
> They deny Him by leaving Him out. Sometimes they deny
> Him by not making Him absolutely central, vital and
> essential. If Christ is not in the centre, He is being denied.
> He is either in the centre or He is nowhere. Again, they
> may deny Him by denying His Person, by regarding Him
> as a man only, as a great teacher, a wonderful example,
> but denying His Deity — denying Him as God-Man, the

'theanthropos', in all the glory and fulness of His blessed Person. Or they deny Him most of all and most seriously by denying His atoning work, by denying the fact that if He had not gone to the cross every man would remain doomed and under the wrath of God, by denying that this is the only way to God, by failing to see themselves as hopeless, damned sinners who are only saved because He bore their sins in His own body on the cross — denying the centrality of the cross! 'denying the Lord that bought them'. Whatever teaching a man may have to offer to you, if the Christ on Calvary's Cross is not the central pivot at the heart of it, I say he is a false prophet and a false teacher. And no one can give hope, either to the individual or to the world today, who is not centred absolutely upon that atonement. He is a false prophet and teacher.[15]

Persuasive preaching

His view of 'Calling for Decisions' is set out in chapter 14 of *Preaching and Preachers*. It was never his practice to issue an appeal, his reasons being: (1) his belief that it is wrong to place the will under direct pressure; (2) that when too much pressure is applied, the various psychological factors become more influential than the truth itself; (3) that the calling for decisions should not be separated from the preaching of the Word of God; (4) the erroneous implication that 'sinners have an inherent power of self-decision and self-conversion'; (5) the implication likewise that the evangelist can somehow manipulate the Holy Spirit and his work; (6) the fact that such a process may only produce a superficial conviction of sin; (7) that by so doing, it encourages people to think that this act of going forward saves them; (8) that it ultimately means a distrust of the Holy Spirit; (9) that regeneration is solely and entirely — like the conviction of sin and the gift of faith — the work of the Holy Spirit; and finally (10) because no sinner ever really 'decides' for Christ. Rather, in MLl-J's words, he 'flies' to Christ, utterly helpless and despairing. It was never his custom therefore to make 'altar calls'. Instead he believed that the persuasiveness of his preaching

was implicit — and cumulative — as the exegesis unfolded and
progressed. Put another way, the total effect of argument,
illustrations from the Bible, the logical outworking of the great
doctrines of Christianity, and his sheer delight in the 'glorious
gospel', constituted an appeal in themselves. Indeed an appeal,
as a separate act, was unnecessary; because what was required
of his congregation in terms of responsibility and commitment,
both from Christians and non-Christians alike, had been made
obvious long before the end of the sermon. Argument and
analysis then, together with the use of the rhetorical question
at a crucial point, of which one example must suffice:

> *Well, what was that gospel*? Just this, that Jesus Christ,
> is the Son of God, that in dying He fulfilled the Law and
> destroyed the power of death, and that by so doing He
> cancelled the power of sin and wiped out the sinful debt
> of humanity and that by the power of His Spirit a man
> can be created anew and start upon a new life which is
> an eternal life. How can I be happy and be free with the
> load of all my past sins upon me? How can I answer this
> voice within me that mocks and taunts me while I am still
> conscious of my guilt? But when I see and believe that
> Christ has taken it upon Himself to deal with my sins,
> when I know that I am forgiven by God through Christ,
> when I know my past sins are blotted out, — let all the
> devils mock and laugh, let all the voices within me and
> in hell jeer and attempt to enslave me — I know I am free
> and can turn upon them. I know their power, thousands
> of times have I experienced it, but God be praised, I now
> know a greater power. I know a power that can lead
> captivity captive, a power that has swallowed up death and
> the grave 'in victory'. My past is clear and I am free.[16]
> (My italics.)

Practical preaching

As has already been illustrated, he constantly emphasized the importance of doctrine, but it was never doctrine in a vacuum. His constant aim was to bring men and women to God, and then to maturity 'in Christ'. He promoted practical holiness by helping Christians to grow in the 'knowledge of the Lord Jesus Christ', to understand truth and then to apply it in their daily lives. In a sermon entitled 'The Salt of the Earth', he defined the Christian's function in society:

> It seems to be that the first thing which is emphasized by our Lord is that one of the Christian's main functions with respect to society is a purely negative one. Now what is the function of salt? There are those who would say that it is to give health, that it is health- or life-giving. But that seems to me to be a serious misunderstanding of the function of salt. Its business is not to provide health; it is to prevent putrefaction. The principal function of salt is to preserve and to act as an antiseptic. Take, for instance, a piece of meat. There are certain germs on its surface, perhaps in its very substance, which have been derived from the animal, or from the atmosphere, and there is the danger of its becoming putrid. The business of the salt which is rubbed into that meat is to preserve it against those agencies that are tending to its putrefaction. Salt's main function, therefore, is surely negative rather than positive. Now clearly this is a very fundamental postulate. It is not the only function of the Christian in the world, because, as we shall see later, we are also to be the light of the world, but in the first instance this is to be our effect as Christians.[17]

But unlike many other evangelicals, he did not advocate that a Christian should not vote, because he considered it the Christian's duty to play his or her role as an individual in society; though he was adamant that it was not the church's role to intervene in social, economic and political matters. But as citizens, Christians could have an indirect influence as salt in society:

Think of great men, like the Earl of Shaftesbury and others, who, as private Christians and as citizens, worked so hard in connection with the Factory Acts. Think also of William Wilberforce and all that he did with regard to the abolition of slavery. As Christians we are citizens of a country, and it is our business to play our part as citizens, and thereby act as salt indirectly in innumerable respects. But that is a very different thing from the Church's doing so.[18]

Ultimately, however, the supreme purpose of his preaching was to produce men and women whose lives did in a real way 'glorify' God.

Systematic preaching

During his years at Westminster Chapel, MLl-J went verse-by-verse through such epistles as Romans (preached on Friday evenings from October 1955 to March 1968) and Ephesians (preached on Sunday mornings between 1954 and 1962). These expositions had a tremendous appeal for an age of doubt and uncertainty about the relevance and appeal of preaching. They touched the hearts and minds of their original hearers, and they continue to do so today in printed form and, of course, as cassette recordings. Sir Frederick Catherwood made this observation:

Although sermons are notoriously unpublishable today, all the volumes in these series sell well throughout the English-speaking world, showing that there is a real demand for reasoned, analytical and applied Bible exposition. He had many letters from all corners of the earth. One day, for example, he was visited by the Rev. Chuck Smith of Calvary Church, Costa Mesa, California, who told him that the books had transformed his preaching. He had once driven himself into mental breakdown trying to use his personality to put over the message. Since then he had let the Bible speak for itself and said that both his ministry and his own health had benefited enormously. What he did not say was that his Sunday morning congregation was then up to 24,000![19]

Spirit-filled preaching

That his preaching had the unction and anointing of the Holy Spirit is self-evident; or to use the language of chapter 16 of *Preaching and Preachers*, it was the 'demonstration of the Spirit and of power'. He defined the anointing of the Spirit like this:

It is the Holy Spirit falling upon the preacher in a special manner. It is an access of power. It is God giving power, and enabling, through the Spirit, to the preacher in order that he may do this work in a manner that lifts it up beyond the efforts and endeavours of man to a position in which the preacher is being used by the Spirit and becomes the channel through whom the Spirit works.[20]

During MLl-J's last-but-one sermon, preached at Ashford Congregational Church, Middlesex, on 4th June 1980, he said:

'Although the preacher may be a small and a feeble man, if he's filled with the Spirit there is a power in him that can bring men and women to conviction of sin, can open their eyes to see their darkness and their lost estate, and can give them faith and capacity to believe'.[21]

The above characteristics could be added to in many other and diverse ways, but they seem to me to represent the essential quality of his preaching. Doubtless some readers will have noticed the absence of any reference to Calvin, for MLl-J was a convinced Calvinist with an immense influence on evangelicalism; but this approach is easily justified by the fact that he did not refer, as such, to the five 'TULIP' points of Calvinism[22]. An alternative explanation is provided by the fact that his theological explanations were not abstruse or overtly technical. They were above all balanced, fluent, and pastoral.

The Puritans too were an important influence on his thinking and on the form of his sermons. Like them, he felt that preaching was central to the whole work of the church and that it should be governed by theology. This was of course reflected by the

Puritans in their definitions of the church and its nature. To them
the first 'mark' was the preaching of the Word of God, followed
by the administration of the sacraments, and finally the carrying
out of discipline. Faithful exposition of the Word of God was,
in their view, the biblical way of promoting holiness.

Sermonic structure

Finally, what of the structure of 'the Doctor's' sermons?

> My training in medicine and surgery are always with me.
> I look at a text, diagnose the condition and decide where
> I am to make the first incision. I cut deep through the layers
> of the tissue until I reach the heart of the problem. I deal
> with it and then rebuild and sew up.

This was the illuminating reply the Revd. Raymond Norman
received in the 1940s when as a student at the Western College,
Bristol (a Congregational College) he asked MLl-J for advice
and guidance in sermon preparation. The medical metaphor he
used is a most apt and constructive starting-point for a brief
comment on the structure of his sermons, two examples of which
will be considered.

1: 'So Great Salvation' – Hebrews 2:1-3*

A: *An initial statement about its nature*
He defines the greatness of salvation in terms of the health,
the wholeness it bestows. He shows how this greatness is
expressed in four areas:
   a) Hymnology: reference is made to Charles Wesley's hymn
'Oh for a thousand tongues to sing', to Samuel Davies's 'Great
God of wonders', and also to Handel's *Messiah*;
   b) Church architecture;
   c) Preaching and oratory;
   d) Art and music.

*Available on cassette from Send the Light Trust, Bromley, Kent.

B: *A detailed analysis of the elements of its greatness*

MLl-J exemplifies it under four heads:

a) *Its authorship*

This principle is operative in literature (Sir Walter Scott), and Art (El Greco): a work is assessed to relation to the person who brought it into being. Salvation, he affirms, is the message of Almighty God. It is not man's message, it is God speaking (Heb. 1:1-4). Salvation was conceived and brought into being by the blessed Holy Trinity.

b) *Because of that from which it saves us*

Salvation delivers us from judgement and death. After death we are assessed by God's standards, his holy law. Our standards don't count. All is failure and defeat, but salvation saves us from eternal punishment: it is the only escape; it imparts peace of conscience, a knowledge of sins forgiven, and all without money and without price.

c) *That for which it saves us*

It (i) reconciles us to God (Heb. 2:17);

(ii) introduces us to God and enables us to speak to and with him;

(iii) gives us a new nature, a new heart, a new outlook, a totally new beginning in life;

(iv) means Jesus is with us, especially in life's extremities;

(v) gives us a vision of the world to come. As heirs of salvation, new heavens and a new earth are being prepared for us.

d) *How it has been prepared for us*

He discusses at length what he calls the 'drama of salvation' as it is centred upon the person of Jesus Christ: the incarnation, the temptation in the wilderness, his atoning death, the resurrection, ascension, and coming again.

C: *A brief conclusion*

Not only is salvation great, it is an incomparable message.

2: 'New Creatures' - 2 Corinthians 5:17*

*Delivered at Send Evangelical Church, 27 May 1975.

A: *Opening remarks*

MLl-J comments on the Pauline method of giving a definition of what it means to be a Christian. He describes it as the most important consideration in the world: it applies to both time and eternity.

B: *Radical change*

Next, MLl-J emphasizes the radical nature of the change when a person becomes a Christian. The difference between a Christian and a non-Christian is as profound a change as it is possible to imagine. It is not something superficial, something added on, an addendum, a varnish: it is something revolutionary. Illustrations of this theme are then given:

John 3:3: 'born again': regeneration;

2 Corinthians 5:17: 'new creatures';

2 Corinthians 4:6: 'light of the knowledge of the glory of God'.

C: *The greatest change of all*

Then he concentrates on the greatest change of all that occurs in a man when he becomes a Christian: in his *thinking and understanding*. The Christian has a totally new way of looking at everything: it's not merely a question of imbibing new ideas. Illustrations of this are taken from 1 Corinthians 2:14ff., Romans 12:1-2, and Ephesians 4:23.

MLl-J then shows that the Christian has an entirely new conception of himself, and this is also demonstrated with particuar reference to:

a) *The life of Paul*

See Philippians 3:4-9, Romans 7:24, and 1 Timothy 1:15.

b) *The experience of Charles Wesley*

'I am all unrighteousness', and 'False and full of sin I am' — such a man despairs of himself, but has complete acceptance 'in' him.

c) *The Lord Jesus Christ*

Many people view him as just a man, but he is in reality the Christ, the Lord of Lords.

d) *Reconciliation*

Only Jesus Christ can reconcile guilty, sinful man to God.

e) *Life in the world*

Shown from 2 Corinthians 5:2. Because of his own internal happiness the Christian is burdened for the world, and he walks through it by faith, trying 'to persuade' men of their lostness. The Christian is thus a journeyman, a stranger and a pilgrim in this world, and seeks for the glory that is to come (2 Cor. 4:17-18).

These bare outlines do scant justice to the vigour of these sermons that was apparent when they were delivered orally. Enough has been adduced, however, to preserve some of the main structural features of MLl-J's sermons:

1. *A brief comment on the dominating theme of the sermon.* In the case of that on 'So Great Salvation', it concerns the first change that occurs when a man becomes a Christian;

2. *Careful definition*;

3. *Detailed exemplification*;

4. *Concluding statement*: no appeal as such, rather the implication built up cumulatively and powerful throughout the sermon, that to reject this message is folly. In all of these sections the illustrations are drawn, almost exclusively, from the Bible.

We can sum up this first aspect of MLl-J's significance by saying that in his sermons we observe the pastor who preached Christ, the shepherd who fed God's flock, the teacher who expounded the Word of life, the watchman who gave warnings, and the evangelist who persuaded men to believe. Put another way, his sermons fulfilled a famous nineteenth-century dictum: 'The power of the minister is in his living relationship with God and his capacity to act as a connecting link between God and the human soul. It is God in the soul which is the secret of true pulpit power.'

THE PASTOR

There is a tendency with some people to think of him just as a preacher. But this is an unbalanced and inadequate explanation of his ministry which, in a very real sense, was pastorally orientated. In South Wales, for example, he lived in a radically different community from that of London and Westminster Chapel, and he was frequently called upon to deal with a range of social, economic, political and medical problems.

At Westminster Chapel too his advice was required by an endless stream of people seeking guidance, comfort, consolation, and encouragement. Significantly at the Thanksgiving Service on Monday 6 April 1981, a senior deacon at Westminster began his tribute by referring to MLl-J as 'my beloved Pastor and Friend', and then added:

> Somebody said that his sermons were all symphonies. I can't think of a better description of them. He stated the theme, and then he repeated it again and again with variations, and at last the sermon culminated in an overwhelming conviction of the truth that he was exploring and expounding.
>
> I took great notice of what happened as a result of these symphonies. You've heard already of the wealth of conversions. I was in a position to see these conversions. They used to come along the passage to the vestry like wounded birds. But he had time for them in the vestry. Indeed I sometimes said he had more time in the vestry than he had in the pulput, and he didn't stint his time here! And this stream of conversions was continual. It characterised the whole of his ministry. He never despised anyone, no matter how weak or feeble, he always encouraged them.[23]

In his 'Reflections' on MLl-J's ministry, the Revd. Edwin King said this:

> The Chapel has often been discussed as nothing more than a preaching centre, yet nothing was further from the truth. Behind the scenes in the week, and after the public services, the number of persons waiting for an interview was always substantial. Though weary with preaching, the Doctor would patiently see them all. If you were but paying

your respects, then very courteously but firmly you were steered towards and out of the vestry door when your time was up. But if you were a soul in need, then time was no object.[24]

His pastoral care extended far beyond the chapels in which he ministered. In Wales, for example, he was a friend and adviser to a large number of ministers, many of whom were struggling to present historic Christianity against a background of doubt, liberalism, and even downright hostility. They got from him wise counsel — balanced and thoughtful — and of course the benefit of his long experience. If they needed a bulwark, someone to lean on, MLl-J was that man. One result of his efforts in Wales was the formation of 'The Evangelical Movement of Wales'. He continued to make preaching forays into Wales throughout his life, preaching to immensely large congregations. To some places, for example Carmarthen, he returned year after year.[25] It was his usual custom to preach in Welsh in the afternoon and in English in the evening. The people who flocked to hear him came from all denominations: Presbyterian, Baptists, Plymouth Brethren, Church of Wales, Methodists, thus amply proving the point that true preaching of the gospel transcends mere denominational barriers and taboos.

But in spite of all this, it is undeniably true that Wales could have had the benefit of his preaching and wisdom on a much fuller and more permanent basis. By this I mean the period towards the end of his ministry in Aberavon, when it was suggested that he be offered a position at the Presbyterian Church of Wales's Theological College at Bala. This was remarkable for a layman without theological training. The South Wales association endorsed this proposal but the North Wales association kept delaying its decision, influenced in part by his lack of formal ministerial training and in part by his conservative theological position. Instead, as we know, he accepted Dr. Campbell Morgan's invitation to become Co-Pastor at Westminster Chapel. This was a controversial time in his life,[26] but with the benefit of hindsight it is possible to declare unreservedly that God's controlling hand was in it all, and his removal to London meant that his influence could be felt more easily and centrally throughout Britain (not just Wales), and indeed the whole world. There was no question of MLl-J having neglected Wales or forgotten its people. It was rather the case that the theological bureaucrats did not welcome his brand of preaching and teaching.

In other areas too his pastoral care and interest was significant, the 'Westminster Fellowship of preachers' being a notable example. Beginning in the early 1940s, it met monthly on Tuesday afternoons, with new members being nominated by existing members. Its numbers grew steadily over the years, and though at first the church parlour was sufficiently large to house all the members by the 1950s a move to the Institute Hall was necessary, and eventually the number of members grew to about 400 names in the 1960s when the day for the meeting was switched to Monday. John Caiger has said that at these gatherings MLl-J impressed them all with his deep spirituality; there was also the definite feeling that MLl-J really enjoyed the meetings.

> The Doctor was in his element in the chair at these sessions. He was a phenomenon. The extraordinary range and precision of his memory, his ability to grasp the essential elements of a subject and to comprehend and reproduce the varying views which were being expressed, his sense of humour (I have seen him literally shaking with laughter in his chair), the swiftness of his repartee, and the skill with which he could sum up a discussion and conclude with exhortations or warnings or encouragements drawn from it, combined to give him a unique place in the respect and affection of the many who hurtled along the various motorways from surprisingly remote parts early on a Monday morning to be with him.[27]

THE MINISTER TO STUDENTS

The history of the Inter-Varsity Fellowship (now U.C.C.F.) began in 1919 after the ending of the hostilities with Germany and her allies. 'The Doctor' spoke first to an I.V.F. conference in 1935 when he was still a minister in South Wales, but it was during the Second World War that he became a dominating force within this student movement.

Even before the war itself had started he was present at the Cambridge International Student Conference from 27 June to 2 July 1939. Over 800 overseas students from 33 different countries came together, with Lord and Lady Kinnaird as host and hostess, to discuss the theme of 'Christ our freedom'; a most apposite subject considering the prevailing international situation at that time. When British students joined them about 1,000 people gathered together for the main sessions. Douglas Johnson, in his volume on the history of the evangelical movement in the universities and colleges, has made this comment on the 1939 conference:

> There was a great spirit of expectancy and enthusiasm ran high. There were many useful exchanges of view and a great deal of purposeful planning was done between the sessions. Perhaps the most encouraging sign of progress was the way in which even small national movements were planning to send deputations of students to the universities in their neighbouring countries. Several of the larger movements were discussing exchanges of deputations on the model set by the recent British parties.[28]

In 1941 and 1942 the I.V.F. conference was held at Trinity College, Cambridge, and MLl-J's Presidential Address on both occasions was attended by Sir G.M. Trevelyan, the Master of the College. At one theological conference MLl-J distinguished himself by the brilliancy of his dialogue with D.R. Davies (formerly a Communist, but subsequently converted to Christianity) in the Senior Common Room at Trinity.

In print too he was able to influence student views. The Graduates Fellowship decided to send a letter bearing the title *The Graduates Fellowship Newsletter* to all ex-members of the various unions, and it included a message from MLl-J.

In 1947 he became the first chairman of the Executive Committee, and then President, of the International Fellowship of Evangelical Students (I.F.E.S.). Towards the end of August 1947 he chaired the International General Committee in Harvard University. In 1951 he conducted a mission at Oxford with Hugh Gough. In 1958 his booklet, *Authority*, was published by Inter-Varsity Fellowship.

Douglas Johnson pin-points MLl-J's distinctive contribution to the I.V.F. and the world of students in general:

> Over many years Dr. Lloyd-Jones gave an astonishing amount of time in speaking at university missions, open meetings, conferences, leading discussions and advising. Both in the pulpit and conference hall he provided a powerful example of fidelity in the truth and concentration on what matters most, which he advocated in personal counsel.[29]

His preaching and counsel also helped to foster the growth of conferences in Wales. He was able to utilize the confidence both North and South Wales had in him to give the students all the possible help he could. Undoubtedly too he was an inspiring leader to Welsh theological college students and graduates in general. I well recall the ferment and excitement one of his visits caused when he came to Cardiff in 1964. When the suggestion was made that the Christian Unions of Wales[30] would profit from an annual conference, he was chosen to speak; and for three years he delivered the chief conference addresses.

There were three particular emphases in his sermons to the students: the vital importance of doctrine; the need to be uncompromising in presenting the great biblical truths; and the necessity of judging everything in the light of the Word of God. To be biblical in thinking and methodology and argument was his perennial message: unthinking Christianity was anathema to him. It's not an exaggeration to say, with Oliver Barclay, that he was 'a great leader throughout the evangelical student world'. His influence continued to be exercised almost to the end of his ministry at Westminster, for in 1963-64 he was again — after a gap of eleven years — President of the Fellowship.

His willingness to give many hours of his valuable time to students in this unstinting manner was typical of his desire to foster the faith of those with whom he came into contact. It also confirms one of the great facets of his ministry: *its pastoral intent*. He was never merely academic (although his mind was as sharp as any university don or teacher) or theoretical; he was always concerned with getting people — not just students — to think properly and spiritually and biblically. This dictum he applied to whatever subject was being discussed: economics, theology, society, history, politics. As a member of the student body for six years in the 1960s, I recall the inspiration he gave to evangelicals; this was particularly so because of the feeling that he was preaching and arguing about matters he had first of all experienced for himself; they were issues he had thought through always from a biblical standpoint — from first principles. He would not let anyone get away with shoddy or sloppy argument, and that is something which appeals to students. He never tailored his message to suit academic or university audiences, as his own reminiscence makes perfectly clear:

I shall never forget preaching some twenty-seven years ago at a college chapel in the University of Oxford on a Sunday morning. I had preached in exactly the same way as I would have preached anywhere else. The moment the service had finished, and before I had scarcely had time to get down from the pulpit, the wife of the Principal came rushing up to me and said, 'Do you know, this is the most remarkable thing I have known in this chapel.' I said, 'What do you mean?' 'Well,' she said, 'do you know that you are literally the first man I have ever heard in this chapel who has preached to us as if we were sinners.' She added, 'All the preachers who come here, because it is a college chapel in Oxford, have obviously been taking exceptional pains to prepare learned, intellectual sermons, thinking we are all great intellects. To start with, the poor fellows often show that they do not have too much intellect themselves, but they have obviously been straining in an

attempt to produce the last ounce of learning and culture,
and the result is that we go away absolutely unfed and
unmoved. We have listened to these essays and our souls
are left dry. They do not seem to understand that though
we live in Oxford we are nevertheless sinners.' Now that
was a statement of fact by a highly intelligent lady, the
wife of the Principal of a college.[31]

But he would never agree to debate 'God' before a university
audience because he believed — and he was surely right — that
'God is not a subject for debate, because He is Who He is and
What He is.' It was this belief that led him in 1942, for example,
to turn down an invitation to debate the question of religion at
the Union Debating Society at Oxford with Dr. C.E.M. Joad.
A number of other people felt he was wrong to turn down a
wonderful opportunity for preaching and presenting the gospel,
but he remained totally convinced that such occasion only
provide 'entertainment', and he discounted it as an effective
means of winning people to the Christian faith.

CHAPTER 4

Controversy

'The Doctor' was considered by many people to be a controversial figure. This was hardly surprising, given the type of man he was and the views he held. He had an incisive mind, preached the Word of God fearlessly, and refused categorically to water down the essential truths of the gospel. His approach to any issue was analytical, logical, and biblical. In addition, he had the consummate skill of the practised debater, though he was not interested in mere point-scoring — the matters he spoke about were far too serious for that. On the other hand, he never shied away from potential areas of controversy, even though by so doing he was severely criticized and often misrepresented. Reference may be made to four subjects in particular.

LARGE-SCALE EVANGELISTIC CRUSADES

Before coming directly to the historical incidents themselves, it is as well to turn to certain emphases in *Preaching and Preachers*. This will enable us to see that his response to large evangelistic crusades was consistent with his whole conception

of preaching. He saw preaching as part of the balanced, daily
life of the church, and not something which is given greater
prominence for limited periods only. For this reason he would
distance himself from those campaigns which he viewed as
isolated, one-off occurrences. The relevant chapter is the ninth
('Calling for Decisions'), which is a most wide-ranging and
comprehensive treatment of the subject. To MLl-J, the emphasis
on music which developed mid-way through the nineteenth
century was simply part of the 'respectability and pseudo-
intellectualism of the Victorians'. From this tendency arose, he
felt, the danger of 'organist tyranny', or the 'demon of the singing',
because of the sheer multiplicity of choirs, especially in Wales.
He also says this:

> I contend that we can lay it down as a fairly general rule
> that the greater the amount of attention that has been paid
> to this aspect of worship — namely the type of building,
> and the ceremonial, and the singing, and the music — the
> greater the emphasis on that, the less spirituality you are
> likely to have; and a lower spiritual temperature and
> spiritual understanding and desire can be expected. But
> I would go further and ask a question, for I feel it is time
> we began to ask this question. As I have said previously
> in another connection, we must break into certain bad
> habits that have settled into the life of our churches and
> which have become a tyranny. I have referred to the set-
> form, and to the people who are ready to play about with
> the Truth and try to modify it, but who resist any change
> in the service and this rigid set-form. So I suggest that
> it is time we asked the question: Why is any of this accent
> on music necessary? Why does it have any place at all?[1]

He answers his own question in the following way:

> Let us face this question; and surely as we do so we must
> come to the conclusion that what we should seek and aim
> at is a congregation of people singing the praises of God
> together; and that the real function of an organ is to

accompany that. It is to be accompaniment; it is not to dictate; and it must never be allowed to do so. It must always be subservient. I would go so far as to say that the preacher generally should choose the tunes as well as the hymns, because sometimes there can be a contradiction between the two. Some tunes virtually contradict the message of the hymn though the metre may be correct. So the preacher has the right to be in charge of these matters; and he must not surrender this right.[2]

Music, he felt, could be part and parcel of the process of conditioning which he considered to be a disadvantage to the *real* preaching of the gospel. Not for him, either, the 'entertainment element'. Nor could he accept the manipulation of the lights in the building: 'just psychological conditioning'. He felt that all these factors and influences — including making an appeal — could lead to effects which were not brought about by the Truth. To illustrate this he quoted a story which had appeared in the Press:

A certain evangelist in Britain had been asked to conduct a programme of hymn singing on a Sunday night on the radio. The programme was a regular Sunday programme lasting for half an hour. Different churches are asked to do this week by week. On this particular occasion this well-known evangelist was taking this programme in the Albert Hall in London. It had been planned as usual, months ahead of time. About a week or so before the programme was actually due to take place, another evangelist arrived in London; and on hearing this the British evangelist invited him to preach before the half-hour broadcast of hymn singing. He did so. This visiting evangelist was told that he must stop at a given time because at that moment they would be 'on the air' for the broadcast of the hymn singing. So he preached and finished promptly on time, and then immediately, they were on the air for the half-hour hymn singing. When that had finished, and they were no longer 'on the air', the visiting evangelist made his

customary 'altar call' giving an invitation to people to come
forward. He was interviewed by the Press the next day and,
amongst other questions, he was asked whether he was
satisfied with the result of his appeal. He replied at once
that he was not, that he was disappointed, and that the
number was much smaller than he had been accustomed
to in London as well as in other places. Then he was asked
the obvious question by one of the journalists — To what,
then, did he attribute the fact that the response was
comparatively small on this occasion? Without any hesi-
tation the evangelist answered that it was quite simple, that
unfortunately the half-hour of hymn singing had come in
between the end of his sermon and the giving of the appeal.
That, he said, was the explanation. If only he had been
allowed to give his appeal immediately at the end of the
sermon the result would have been altogether greater.[3]

Further proof of the undesirability, to MLl-J, of certain of these
factors was the admission by various evangelists that only one-
tenth of all 'decisions' for Christ actually lasted. Equally strongly,
he objected to the 'carnality expressing itself as an unhealthy
interest in numbers'. Perhaps even more fundamentally, he saw
the prediction of the number of responses and the results likely
to accrue from big evangelistic crusades as being totally at
variance with the work of the Holy Spirit. In his view, the appeal
of the evangelist must be 'in the Truth itself',[4] and salvation is
peculiarly the work of the Holy Spirit:' His work is a thorough
work, it is a lasting work; and so we must not yield to this over-
anxiety about results'.[5]

A moment's reflection is sufficient to identify some of the
issues above with the crusades conducted by Dr. Billy Graham.
So we come to the year 1954, the year of the Harringay Crusade.
Evangelicals were in a state of high excitement at the prospect
of hundreds of people being converted under the preaching of
Dr. Graham. This was to be *the* great opportunity, the beginning
of the revival, the turning-point after many years of declining
congregations, a new impetus to Christian life and witness in
Britain. It was not an enthusiasm shared by 'the Doctor': mass

evangelism was quite simply not the work he felt he had been called to. His stance led to much criticism[6] by other evangelicals and, doubtless too, loneliness, not least because he was misunderstood by many people.

However, in defence of his response — though to some it may seem like heresy — it is possible to pin-point several problematical areas connected with mass evangelism in a technically orientated, multi-media, publicity-conscious world, whether it be back in the fifties or in the eighties. There is always the problem of merely superficial conversions. Under the pressure of a high-powered organization, persistently alluring — even hypnotic — music, and long appeals, many do respond emotionally, on the spur of the moment, only to fall away soon afterwards. While in the interests of fairness it must be stressed that many real conversions take place in such meetings, it is also true that some converts fade away fairly soon after the initial enthusiasm has waned, particularly if new converts are placed in liberal or lethargic churches where the run-of-the mill life is vastly different from the excitement of huge evangelistic campaigns.

But the very decisiveness of his attitude undoubtedly did cause offence in 1954. Perhaps the most pressing of the problems alluded to above concerns the logistics of putting the new converts in touch with churches. Inevitably, many of them were directed to churches which were not evangelical and thus had scant sympathy for the new-found fervour and zeal of the converts.

Furthermore, the history of Christianity shows that the church progresses and moves forward by true preaching of the Word of God which leads to revival. So the preaching of the gospel must never be seen in isolation, but as part of the continuing work, witness and worship of the church. It must also be observed that over-reliance on some of the extra-curricular factors and methods referred to above is inconsistent with the view that in salvation and regeneration the work of the Holy Spirit is absolutely sovereign: it is his sole work, and his alone.

None of this detracts from the view that Dr. Graham is a marvellous man of God whose preaching has been signally blessed; but it does not follow that all his methods must be

accepted uncritically. Clearly MLl-J felt unhappy about some
of them, and the result was that he did not have any part in the
Harringay Crusade, nor in any of Dr. Graham's subsequent visits
to Britain. He did, however, agree to meet him for a discussion
in his rooms at Westminster Chapel.

TEACHING ON THE WORK OF THE SPIRIT

By this heading is meant his teaching on the 'sealing of the Spirit'.
He expounded this subject at enormous length in two volumes
of his published sermons. One was *Romans — The Sons of God
(8:5-17)*, first published in 1974; these sermons had been
preached on Friday evenings between March 1960 and April
1961. The other was *Ephesians — God's Ultimate Purpose
(chapter 1)*, first published in 1978; these sermons had been
preached on Sunday mornings during the year 1954-55.

Both volumes led to considerable debate among evangelicals
in general and among devotees of 'Reformed' theology in
particular, and continue to do so in the 1980s.

In sermon 21 of the Ephesians volume, after dealing with the
sealing of the Spirit as part of the 'inheritance' of Christians and
comparing the use of the word 'seal' in Ephesians 1:13 with other
scriptures (for example, John 6:27), he posed this crucial
question: 'Where exactly does the sealing come in the life and
experience of the Christian?'

MLl-J's assertion is that the 'sealing with the Spirit' is
something 'subsequent to believing, something additional to
believing' (p.250); something which is 'distinct from believing,
and not part of believing' (p.248). To substantiate his views, he
appealed for support to the seventeenth-century Puritans, Thomas
Goodwin and John Owen, and to the later writers Charles
Simeon and Charles Hodge; and then by reference to a number
of biblical examples: Acts 8 (Philip and the Samaritan), Acts
9 (the conversion of Saul of Tarsus), Acts 15 (the apostle Peter's
defence for admitting Cornelius and his family into the Christian
church), Acts 19 (Paul at Ephesus). His conclusion is that there
is a distinction between believing and sealing, indeed that there

is 'always an interval — that sealing does not immediately and automatically happen at believing'; and he went on to say that 'it may be a short interval, so short as to suggest that the believing and the sealing are simultaneous; but there is always an interval'. His corollary is that it is possible to be a true believer without being sealed; that sealing does not happen inevitably to all who become Christians; in other words, conversion and sealing are *not* identical. In the volume on Romans he does allow that there 'are some instances in which it sealing is almost simultaneous with conversion'. The key word here is 'almost', as he goes on to say:

> But in the light of all the other examples and illustrations we realize that, even there, there must have been belief first — but the interval was a very short one. But in the vast majority of instances there is a clear interval, sometimes there is a long interval. *The important principle is that the two things are always separable.* And surely this is quite inevitable, for, if the Spirit confirms our own spirit, there must therefore have been something that has happened in our spirit first for the Holy Spirit to confirm. You cannot have 'the Spirit of adoption, whereby we cry, Abba, Father', without being a believer. Believing must come first. What the Spirit does is to testify with our spirit. If there was no testimony in our spirit, the Spirit could not confirm it. So it follows, of necessity, from every standpoint — from the plain teaching of Scripture, from the testimonies of men, and from an obvious deduction drawn from the very nature of what is happening — that believing must precede the testimony of the Holy Spirit. (*Romans 8:5-17*, p.318).

Here I have italicized the cardinal part of MLl-J's argument.

The third fundamental statement he made about the Sealing of the Spirit is found in Sermon 22 of the Ephesians volume, to the effect that 'baptism of the Spirit' is the same as the 'sealing with the Spirit' (p.244). In the same sermon he makes a number of negative statements about the nature of the sealing. It is not

the Holy Spirit's work in regeneration, or repentance or faith.
It is not that unction of the Holy Spirit which is designed
specifically for our spiritual understanding (p.261). Nor is it
sanctification, 'which has nothing to do with it in a direct sense.
It is something quite distinct and separate' (p.261). Nor does
it mean that assurance of salvation which is the 'result of our
believing the Word or as the result of arguments worked out from
the Word' (p.262); and lastly it is not the 'fullness of the Spirit'
which is something which 'you and I can control' (p.263).

So the question arises, what *is* the central truth concerning
the Sealing of the Spirit? In the volume on Ephesians 1, he says
that it 'gives the assurance of sonship, and the "Spirit of
Adoption" whereby we cry "Abba, Father" ' (p.281). In his
treatment of Romans 8:16 he defines it in terms of the 'greatest
form of certainty and assurance that one can ever have of the
fact that one is a child of God. At the same time, of course,
it gives a better understanding of the whole plan of salvation;
there is a kind of luminosity with respect to the truth' (p.304).
Later he adds: 'We are given this absolute assurance of God's
love to us, that we are His children, and that He has "loved us
with an everlasting love" '. He sums the whole matter up like this:

> Not only so; this experience may be accompanied by
> various gifts. It was so on the day of Pentecost. I say 'may
> be', however, for there are variations in this respect, and
> there is not an exact repetition each time. It is for this
> reason that those who say that if we have not spoken in
> tongues we have never been baptized with the Spirit are
> utterly unscriptural. The Apostle asks in 1 Corinthians
> 12: 'Do all speak with tongues?' The answer, obviously,
> is 'No'; as all do not work miracles, and so on. In the same
> way, when we look at the subsequent history of the Chris-
> tian Church in the times of great revival when the Spirit
> of God has been poured forth and thousands have been
> baptized with the Spirit, there is generally no mention of
> their working miracles, no suggestion that they 'spake with
> tongues.' Similarly is this true of individuals who have
> experienced this baptism. There may, or may not be,

accompanying gifts. These, then, are variable factors. What is invariable, what is an absolute, is the certainty and assurance of God's love to His own, this knowledge beyond any doubt or question that they are His children. He tells us that Himself: 'The Spirit beareth witness with our spirit, that we are the children of God.' (*Romans 8:5-17*, p.305).

So this assurance may be accompanied by the gifts of the Spirit (for example, working miracles or speaking in tongues), though in fairness he fully recognizes the variable nature of these gifts. Another variable, in his view, is the way in which this experience is communicated to the individual believer. It may come when a Christian is on his or her own quietly reading the Scriptures, and a certain passage appeals in a particularly distinct and remarkable way; it may occur apart from the Scriptures altogether, in which case it is just an 'inner consciousness in the spirit'; it may happen with or without the aid of a preacher. All this is simply a way of illustrating the sovereignty of the Holy Spirit.

For a detailed discussion of this subject readers are directed to Appendix 4.

THE BASIS OF CHRISTIAN UNITY

Some readers will recognize the heading to this section as the title of a booklet by MLl-J published in December, 1962. It contains the substance of two addresses given at a gathering of ministers in June of that year. Ever since the First Congress of the World Council of Churches in Amsterdam in 1948, the question of unity had been a focus of considerable discussion in all branches of the Christian church. The booklet represents MLl-J's response to this.

He begins with a brief introduction reviewing some of the opinions currently held. The Roman Catholic church sought 'absorption into her institutional organisation'. The Greek and Russian Orthodox view was that other branches of the church must return to them as the true church of Christ. Some believed that 'everybody claiming the name of Christian should meet together, should have fellowship together, and present a common front to the enemies of Christianity'. Finally he outlined a notion then current in evangelical circles which regarded 'unity in terms of coming together to form a kind of "forum" where various views of the Christianity faith may be "discussed", and people may present their different "insights" hoping that as a result they may eventually arrive at some common agreement'.

He then proceeds to examine the teaching of John 17 (especially verse 21), and Ephesians 4 (especially verse 13). There are three vitally important questions which must be answered:

First: what is the nature or the character of true unity?
Second: what is the place of doctrine and belief in this matter of unity?
Third: how does unity come into being?

He points out that the unity referred to in John 17 is restricted to a particular group of people:

> These people who are the subjects of the unity of which our Lord is speaking are not those who happen to have been brought up in a certain country, or who happen to belong to a given race or nation or a particular visible church. They are those who have 'received his word', His teaching, and particularly His teaching concerning Himself. They have known who He is, that He has been sent by God, and that He has been sent to do this work for them. They have 'believed' and have 'received' that word. That is His own definition of these people. In other words, the unity of which He is speaking applies only to those who receive and believe this word — what we now would call the gospel message. (p.11).

This unity is not something to be striven for; it is given by God through the work of the Holy Spirit:

> (It) is produced by the operation of the Holy Spirit and the act of regeneration, and shows itself in a common belief

and reception of the teaching concerning our Lord's Person and work. (p.15)

He then analyses Ephesians 4 in some detail. Unlike John 17, which is a prayer addressed to the Father, Ephesians 4:1-16 is an exhortation directed at Christians who need instruction. MLl-J emphasizes that biblical doctrine must be basic for Christian fellowship and evangelism. He concludes:

There is no fellowship among people who are not agreed about the 'one Spirit, the one Lord, the one faith, the one baptism, the one God who is over all'. There is no real fellowship and unity in a group of people where some believe in 'the wrath of God against sin' and that it has already been 'revealed from heaven' (Romans 1:18), and others not only do not believe in the wrath of God at all, but say that it is almost blasphemous to teach such a thing, and that they cannot believe in a God who is capable of wrath. Fellowship exists only among those who believe, as the result of the operation of the Holy Spirit, these essential truths concerning man's lost estate — that we are all 'by nature the children of wrath' (Ephesians 2:3) — and the action of God in Christ Jesus for our salvation and restoration. There is no fellowship between people who believe that and those who believe something else, which they may call a gospel but which, as Paul tells the Galatians, 'is not a gospel' (Galatians 1:6,7). How ridiculous it is to suggest that there can be fellowship and unity between those who believe that they are saved and have access into God's presence solely because in His great love He made His own Son 'to be sin for us' (2 Corinthians 5:21) and spared Him not but delivered Him up for us all (Romans 8:32), and those who believe that the death of Christ was a great tragedy, but that God forgives us even that, and that ultimately we save ourselves by our obedience, good works and our practice of religion. (p.46-47)

In this address MLl-J presents his arguments with the force, warmth and clarity that were characteristic of him. He distances himself, precisely and emphatically, from all whose ideas of unity are not shaped by the twin influences of truth and doctrine. He could not accept that the Christian faith is 'mystical' in the sense that it cannot be analysed or expressed in clearcut statements and propositions. Nor could he tolerate accepting totally diverse views on the ground that they might be 'insights' pointing somehow to an ultimate truth which must be largely unknown. To refrain from exposing error was to shirk the important Christian responsibility of speaking the truth in love.

Ultimately 'the Doctor' saw unity in 'terms of life':

> Unity must obviously never be thought of primarily in numerical terms, but always in terms of life. Nothing is so opposed to the biblical teaching as the modern idea that numbers and powerful organization alone count. It is the very opposite of the great biblical doctrine of the 'remnant', stated, for instance, so perfectly by Jonathan to his armour bearer as they faced alone the hosts of the Philistines, in the words, 'Come, and let us go over unto the garrison of these uncircumcised : it may be that the Lord will work for us : for there is no restraint to the Lord to save by many or by few' (1 Samuel 14:6). Still more strikingly, perhaps, is it taught in the incident of Gideon and the Midianites, where we read of God reducing the army of Israel from 32,000 to 300 as a preliminary to victory (Judges 7). (p.63)

Or as he declared in *Ephesians 4:1-16 : Christian Unity:*

> The unity produced by the Spirit is primarily spiritual, unseen and internal. Of course it expresses itself also visibly and externally, for as Christians we worship together, we belong to churches together and come into contact with one another constantly. But the thing itself is internal. Let us note again the importance of the order. We do not start with that which is external and then hope to arrive at the internal. We start with the internal and then proceed to express it externally. (p.39)

RELATIONS WITHIN EVANGELICALISM

'The Doctor' had an independent mind. He did not fit into any evangelical mould, and consequently his relationships within evangelicalism were not always harmonious. But less than two years before his retirement from Westminster Chapel he came into sharp conflict with large sections of the evangelical world. This occurred at the National Assembly of Evangelicals' meeting at the Central Hall Westminster on 18 October 1966. The Evangelical Alliance had sponsored the meeting, so that he could re-state in public the views and arguments he had previously put in private to the Alliance's commission on church unity.

In order to appreciate the full significance of the meeting, it is necessary to sketch — albeit briefly — some of the background factors, with particular reference to the situation in Wales. By the mid-sixties it was apparent that the historic denominations had forsaken not only their own historic standards, but also large parts of the Truth as revealed in the Bible. At this time a notable Welsh philanthropist, Sir David James, made available a substantial sum of money to the nonconformist denominations, provided they achieved unity within a stipulated period of time. Those with ecumenical interests received this offer enthusiastically, and proposals for church unity were drawn up. Evangelicals, however, were unable to respond with equal enthusiasm. They quickly — and rightly — realized that the new church structures envisaged would embrace such broad-based theological views that they would be forced to reconsider their position within the denominations. Fundamental truths quietly jettisoned over the years were unlikely to be recovered in any organization resulting from the church unity proposals. The situation in England was not very different, with influential people — both lay and cleric — accepting the basic emphases of the Ecumenical movement.

Alongside these factors must be placed MLl-J's growing conviction that evangelicals had, for a long time, paid inadequate attention to the doctrine of the church. As he understood the New Testament teaching, 'the only people who could be guilty of the sin of schism were those who in reality belonged to the body of Christ . . . and yet remained separate from one another in different denominations. They (and they alone) could be guilty of that sin (schism)'.[7] He pointed out too that by remaining within the historic denominations they were recognizing the ministry of men 'who denied their Lord' (his words). In other words, a serious wrong was being committed against the Lord Jesus Christ himself and against his church, the very institution which he had ordained for the good of his people. Another, pressing consideration was the extent to which liberal theology had influenced the existing denominations.

So we come to the October 1966 meeting. Observers have variously described the atmosphere in the auditorium as 'exciting', 'dramatic', 'tense', and 'tension-filled'. Momentous it certainly was, because MLl-J was aiming in his address to persuade evangelicals to think seriously and constructively about 'The Doctrine of the Church'. He felt that the subject was all the more urgent because of the divisions already existing amongst evangelicals, many of whom were preoccupied with preserving their denominational identity, and because of evangelical links with the Ecumenical movement.

'The Doctor' structured his address around two fundamental questions: Firstly, were evangelicals prepared to remain merely as an adjunct of the church? Secondly, what *was* the Christian church? He issued a call to evangelicals to join together, to leave what he considered to be compromised denominations. Only in this way, he argued, could they hold and honour the Truth in reality: an alliance in faith, doctrine, and behaviour, rather than a concern for mere numbers. Part of his concluding argument included this dramatic appeal:

> We are not interested in numbers but in the truth. Go home and read the story of Gideon again, and see how God has acted through one man. If we stand for God's truth we can be sure God will honour and bless us.
>
> Therefore, fellow evangelical Christians, rise to the occasion and listen to the call of God. If we have one objective only, namely, the glory of the Lord, we shall be led by the Spirit to the true answer to these problems.[8]

He completed his remarks and sat down. The Revd. John Stott, Chairman of the meeting, then rose to dissent, in emphatic terms, from what had been said.

Irrespective of the merits or demerits of MLl-J's case, for a chairman to interject in this way was clearly out of order, and 'the Doctor' was not unnaturally disappointed that Stott should have reacted in this manner. Claim and counter-claim followed, and it was later maintained that he had merely *suggested* that evangelicals should be ready to withdraw, while others indicated that he had been waiting for the right moment to issue such a decisive call. Neither of these views is strictly accurate. Later too a rumour circulated that Stott had apologized to MLl-J for his part in the proceedings, but no such apology, to the best of my knowledge has ever been made public. Certainly Stott had a considerable liking and admiration for 'the Doctor' and must have felt the extensive ramifications of that evening quite keenly. Possibly Stott's behaviour was the result of anticipating the wholesale departure of young evangelical clergymen from the Church of England (who might well be influenced by MLl-J's views), so that his response was a strong reaction to this.

Looking back to that October night with the benefit of almost twenty years of hindsight, it seems extraordinary that the Evangelical Alliance invited MLl-J to give the address in public at all. Those responsible must have known what line he would follow. It is indeed possible that the intention was that the airing of his views in a public setting would, because of the resulting furore and controversy, kill off the proposals at birth. One may further speculate that while the views expressed were much what had been expected, his call to quit the tainted denominations went beyond what had been anticipated. If neither the Evangelical Alliance nor John Stott had bargained for this, then one can understand why the latter departed from his role of impartial chairman.

Such an interpretation involves taking an admittedly "political view" of the Alliance's intentions, but the fact remains that his clarion call fell, for the most part, on deaf ears: the baby was indeed still-born. There was no substantial exodus of evangelicals from the historic denominations,[9] and the leaders of the evangelical wing of the Church of England, in particular, rejected firmly MLl-J's equally firmly held views. His call again fell on unresponsive ears when it was repeated at the British Evangelical Council's annual conference.

The result was the very opposite of what he had hoped for. Indeed, in the aftermath to the October meeting some sections of the evangelical world became disaffected with MLl-J's teaching. Against this tendency, however, must be placed three extremely important developments in Wales.

In the first place, new churches gradually emerged which were wholly and vigorously committed to the evangelical faith. Secondly, the Evangelical Movement of Wales sponsored the 'Church Issues Conference' in order to discuss and pray about matters of mutual interest. Thirdly, a four-year theological training course was started in August 1972 for those people who – owing to theological preferences and reasons of conscience – felt unable to attend colleges within the traditional denominations. This course has three constituent parts: two residential weeks each year; a prescribed course of study throughout the year; and, whenever feasible, assistance and instruction from a local pastor. Ten years after this, in 1982, a parallel Welsh language course commenced.

In contrast to these exciting innovations in Wales, opinions of evangelical Anglicans, for example, have not changed during the past two decades. Conclusive proof of this is found in Canon David Watson's autobiography, *You Are My God*, published in 1983. In chapter 11 of this thoroughly admirable work he asserts that if the work of the Holy Spirit in renewal is to be of any significance at all it must 'be worked out within the mainline denominations'. He also declares that God's purpose is to renew 'the dry bones of existing Christian traditions, and we should not try to bypass them in favour of something more immediately exciting'. His overall reasoning is that to create yet another new or independent grouping would be to fragment even further an already sad and depressing situation in which the church has almost 21,000 denominations throughout the world. In the same chapter he records that at St. Michael's York a seemingly paradoxical state of affairs existed: 'We became more consciously

Anglican even though my work was becoming increasingly ecumenical.' He came to the conclusion that the renewing work of the Holy Spirit' was of no value at all if it had no place within the Anglican tradition itself', or indeed 'within any other mainline tradition'. David Watson also found at York that although their basic identity was that of the Anglican liturgy, the congregation discovered ample and refreshing freedom within that form of worship. The basic point here, however, is that Watson's insistence on reform taking place only within the mainline denominations runs directly counter to what 'the Doctor' advocated in October 1966.

These complicated and often distressing issues suggest, by implication, two further but related considerations. First, MLl-J's relations with and influence upon the historic denominations; and secondly, his impact upon evangelicalism in general. The answers to them are not simple to arrive at because of the almost impossible task of quantifying the extent of his influence.

Within the historic denominations, both the traditionalists and liberals admired the intellectual force of his arguments and the passionate oratory of his sermons; but they drew different conclusions from him on a large number of points, not least on the nature of the gospel and of the church itself. From this viewpoint the only tenable conclusion is that his preaching led to no discernible changes in the traditional distinctives of the Anglicans, Baptists, Methodists, and others, nor in the force of their special emphases.

The same is probably true of evangelicalism in general. His preaching gave immense encouragement to the Fellowship of Independent Evangelical Churches (F.I.E.C.), founded in 1922 by the Revd. E.J. Poole-Connor. Yet at the same time, as has already been shown, evangelicals did not follow his call to come together to form a new grouping, a fact which probably caused 'the Doctor' considerable disappointment in old age.

It is also relevant to refer to his links with the Plymouth Brethren who did historically in the nineteenth century what MLl-J was advocating in the twentieth. His first (and somewhat curious) introduction to the Brethren occurred at Llanelli in 1929. While staying in the town for Christmas, members of the local

Open Brethren Assembly presented him with a Scofield Bible
and, in Murray's words, 'encouraged him to note the importance
of prophetic beliefs'.[10] His lack of enthusiasm must have
surprised them not a little. More pertinently perhaps, Professor
F. F. Bruce, the movement's best-known and ablest scholar,
remembers sitting in a common-room at a convention and noting
'the Doctor' deep in conversation with several men who were
unhappy about their church affiliations, and explaining to them
his concept of leaving the denominations and forming a new
evangelical grouping. Suddenly he turned to Bruce and asked,
'Why don't you (the Brethren) come in with us on this? Together
we could make something worthwhile of it.' This reminiscence
is something of a corrective to the conjecture common among
the Brethren that 'the Doctor' did not consider them to be quite
'spot-on' as far as he understood the faith. Perhaps what he did
not fully realize is that it is impossible for the Brethren to take
any united or ecclesiastical action, since such an ecclesiastical
existence is restricted to the local church. Each Brethren church
is independent, self-governing. No central machinery links them
together or relates them to each other. It may be significant,
therefore, that MLl-J made no reference to them in his October
1966 address.

But he did have a considerable impact on a number of
individuals among the Brethren. Large numbers of them
regularly attended his Sunday evening services at Westminster
Chapel, as did many others who found themselves in London
over the weekend. They did so because they appreciated his
robustly uncompromising presentation of the fundamentals of
the faith. When, however, he expressed opinions which the
Brethren felt to be inconsistent with their own, or when he
pronounced on subjects they considered to be non-essential to
the faith, they were quite simply prepared to differ from him.
The most serious divergence between 'the Doctor' and the
Brethren concerns his teaching on the Baptism with the Spirit.

As someone reared and brought up within Brethren assemblies
in Wales, I can vouch for the immediacy of his impact, and for
the tremendous encouragement his preaching of the gospel gave
me when pursuing my 'A' level studies at school, and even more

so while at university. The cynicism and lessening of standards so evident in the 'swinging sixties' foundered on the rock-like certainty his ministry imparted to me. The same was true for many of the Christians of my generation.

What conclusions can be drawn from all of this, almost twenty years on from that controversial October night?

On a personal level, MLl-J's courage has to be admired. He was prepared to put forward views on an extremely controversial subject to people who were not, for the most part, committed to a similar viewpoint. He argued his case comprehensively and vigorously. Undoubtedly some of the responses to what he had to say saddened him and made him feel lonely and isolated. A noticeable feature of the whole affair – as with others previously in his life – was his ability to remain friendly with those who disagreed fundamentally with him and he with them. Inevitably, in the aftermath to that watershed evening, entrenched positions were adopted, myths circulated widely, and unnecessarily harsh opinions were delivered. One such myth (a politer word would be 'misnomer') was that his views were primarily anti-Anglican. This was not true. What he was arguing against was the 'comprehensivist' idea of the church as a large umbrella-like organism, sufficiently broad-based to embrace people of *totally divergent* opinions. 'The Doctor' contended that for evangelicals to remain within such a body was to neglect the New Testament teaching on the nature and function of the church.

Another misunderstanding existed regarding the timing of any secession. Some assumed that MLl-J meant either an immediate withdrawal or at least within a very short space of time. This is not what he had in mind at all. Nor did he see seceding as an 'across-the-board' matter. Rather, to him it was something to be approached patiently, tolerantly, and of course honourably. In fact, he saw it primarily in terms of educating people within the churches, acquainting them fully with the New Testament teaching on the subject, so that gradually they would realize the implications of that teaching and be prepared to act upon it.

He stressed the need for a 'one step at a time' approach; and he insisted that ministers and lay people thinking of leaving their denominations should conduct negotiations in an attitude of brotherly Christian love: it should most definitely not be a case of 'them' and 'us'. He felt too that where property was involved the relevant business matters should be carried out with friendliness, politeness and, whenever, possible, without being caught up in acrimonious legal transactions. It is obvious now that a number of the resulting problems could have been avoided had people really understood what MLl-J had in mind. Nor were all able to appreciate that he was, above all, concerned with the truth, as he conceived it.

Whatever the rights and wrongs of the various arguments pronounced twenty years ago, it is a salutary exercise to ponder the state of the traditional denominations and evangelicalism today. In the former there is, in many instances, the continuing subservience of biblical truth to denominational prejudices and customs, with decreasing numbers attending both nonconformist and Anglican churches on a regular basis. Also, evangelicals who have remained within the historic denominations are increasingly finding themselves in a muddle: strong tensions exist with regard to both truth and its practice. Many evangelicals too are dispirited as they observe the relentless march of liberal theology in Britain. Added to these factors is the continued tarrying of revival (another thing MLl-J constantly prayed about and hoped for), though this last fact is periodically obscured by the arrival of prominent evangelists from Europe and the United States for large-scale missions in this country. Evangelism, of course, is not revival,[11] as 'the Doctor' — and we — know only too well.

MLl-J's prophetic call went largely unheeded in 1966. In 1986 it retains, for me, its soundness and consistency with biblical truth.

CHAPTER 5

Some Personal Viewpoints

This is not an academic — let alone an official — biography. Nor is it intended as an uncritical eulogy of a great man. But it is important to recognise that 'the Doctor' had an influence on individuals which was both immense and enduring. This chapter contains some 'case histories' which must be typical of many.

1

For the first of these personal viewpoints I turned to the *Revd. Derek Moon*, minister of Godalming (Queen Street) Baptist Church, Surrey. For a short time in the late 1940s he had attended a Bible class organized and conducted at Westminster Chapel by one of the members. This incidental and fringe link with the Chapel, and thus with MLl-J, was taken a significant step further when Derek heard a tape of his sermon on Ephesians 1:13: 'In whom ye also trusted after that ye heard the word of truth, the gospel of your salvation: in whom also after that ye believed, ye were sealed with the Holy Spirit of promise'.[1] The exposition of this verse impressed Derek deeply, and he now fully realized that he needed to become a Christian. He did so, and within a week he had also experienced the baptism with the Holy Spirit.

During the following two years he attended Westminster Chapel and profited enormously from the consistent expository ministry there. He discussed with 'the Doctor' his conversion and also his plans and intentions for the future. Thus Friday nights and Sundays were times of instruction, knowledge, and an increasing awareness and understanding of Christian doctrine. Like his mentor, he came to see that conduct and doctrine cannot be separated, indeed that they are indispensable to each other: a combination of faith and works. Later, during the early 1960s, Derek received an invitation to become the assistant minister at a new Baptist church, Leigh Park, Havant, Hants, where he was ordained in January 1963. Not only did MLl-J give him wise spiritual advice at this time, but he was also one of the signatories to Derek's application form to the Baptist Union. Links with MLl-J were perpetuated in other ways too, though mainly through the Westminster Fellowship. Asked about his dominating impressions of 'the Doctor', Derek referred to six factors.

His tremendous authority in preaching: 'It gave confidence to young Christians, students, mature Christians, and also to ministers, when to admit to being an evangelical was not a popular thing to do. This authority was the direct result of MLl-J's disciplined and unstinting reading of the Word of God.'

His consistent emphasis on the importance of Truth: 'To MLl-J, the only defence and safeguard against error was the abiding truth of the Scriptures.'

His ability as a great encourager of people: 'This was particularly true for those going through a hard time, be it spiritually, emotionally, or psychologically.'

His life as an example to other Christians: 'His life was notable for its discipline, dedication, and consistency.'

His stress on spiritual thinking: 'This was a process in which the Word of God was of fundamental importance. In the Westminster Fellowship he would not let people get away with woolly or illogical or sloppy thinking.'

His qualities as a man of God: 'MLl-J was not just a preacher. He was in every sense a man of God, who was always sincere, single-minded, and courageous. He was prepared to endure the loneliness that inevitably accompanied his stand on church unity, and his refusal to associate himself with the Billy Graham campaigns.'

In addition, Derek referred to his phenomenal memory, quick repartee, and the fact that his life was bound together into a cohesive whole by an exceedingly happy marriage.

2

For a representative from the academic world I approached the *Revd. Clement Connell*, now living in retirement in Cranleigh, Surrey. After reading Classics at Cambridge, there followed two years at Regent's Park College, Oxford, preparing for the Baptist ministry. Clement was subsequently a minister for fifteen years: ten of them at Rayner's Hill, Harrow, followed by five at Herne Hill Baptist Church, South London. He then spent twenty-five years at London Bible College, as a lecturer in Biblical Theology, New Testament, and Greek Testament, as well as being Director of Studies for twenty-four of those years. Clement's viewpoint is slightly different from Derek's in that he was already a mature and experienced Christian when he came under MLl-J's influence. He was a member of the Westminster Fellowship for twenty years, from 1942-62; he became secretary of the Fellowship about 1945-6. So he is a witness from the war days right through to the last six years of 'the Doctor's' years at Westminster Chapel.

Clement recalled that when he first joined the Fellowship as a young minister the meetings occurred monthly, beginning at 1.30pm, with a total membership of about twenty or thirty ministers. The number at this time was quite deliberately limited, for two main reasons: firstly so that the fellowship would not get too big; and secondly so that people with insistently controversial views would not be invited to join. At the start of the meeting members made some comments on matters of biblical interest, or shared their difficulties, and then after a short break for a cup of tea, members agreed on a theme to be discussed in more detail. He said that MLl-J was 'masterly' in guiding these discussions (something Professor F.F. Bruce also noticed about him at Inter-Varsity Fellowship conferences too), without directly stating his views on the subject being analysed. This was so 'despite the fact that "the Doctor" knew absolutely what he believed', and also the direction in he wished to guide the members, so that the right conclusions might be drawn. Clement pointed out that the members were perfectly free to disagree with MLl-J, and that he himself acted as a 'devil's advocate' in order to stimulate the conversation.

'The Doctor' also visited Clement's church in South London to preach, and later he preached at the opening of the new buildings at London Bible College. On that occasion he stressed the need for maintaining the evangelical foundations of the faith. This is how Clement conceived of the influence MLl-J exercised:

> The value and significance of the Westminster Fellowship was two-fold. Firstly, there was the help he gave in regard to the practice of the ministry. He knew from experience the complex problems (both in situations and relationships) that arise in the course of everyday ministry, and so he was well able to give practical assistance to young ministers, something which they greatly appreciated. Then secondly there were the insights he brought to many passages of Scripture, which of course he had pondered seriously and carefully over the years. 'The Doctor' strengthened the evangelical faith that people already had, and he was responsible for introducing many people to the pathway of faith, notably members of the student body in England and Wales through the Inter-Varsity Fellowship.

Clement could not, however, go all the way with him on all aspects of his teaching, especially in the crucial area of the Sealing of the Spirit. He also felt that the October 1966 call to evangelicals was both 'unreasonable and unrealistic'.

This is how Clement summed up his impressions:

> As a man 'the Doctor' was friendly, gracious, even-

tempered, displaying an equanimity that was apparent even
when he was opposed vigorously in argument.

As a preacher he was unique in the way he developed the
meaning of a passage or a key text, especially as it applied
to real-life situations: it was never merely exegesis.

As a pastor and counsellor he was understanding and
unfailingly helpful, always ready to assist with personal
problems, or with inexperienced ministers going through
difficulties in their churches.

3

For a Welsh view of 'the Doctor' I was delighted to be able
to consult the *Revd. Vernon Higham*, who has been minister of
Heath Evangelical (formerly Presbyterian) Church for the past
twenty-four years. His recollections go right back to childhood,
when his parents used to talk about a preacher who drew large
audiences to the Free Trade Hall, Manchester — at this time
the Higham family lived in Bolton, having previously lived in
Caernarfon. MLl-J's name was held in high respect, but it was
as a student (at Trinity College, Carmarthen) in 1946 that Vernon
first heard him preach. He was deeply disturbed by the message
(on Dagon and the Ark), and his serious quest for God had
begun. Later, while at theological college in Aberystwyth,
Vernon was converted.

He now needed someone to turn to for advice and direction,
and so his next encounter with 'the Doctor' was a most
encouraging one. It occurred at Llanelli (in 1956) when he was
asked to read the Scriptures and pray before the sermon was
delivered. Coming down from the pulpit MLl-J addressed him
thus: 'You helped me, my boy.' From such a distinguished figure
this was praise indeed. The link forged in this was to continue
until the very end of MLl-J's life.

Vernon also recalled the day (in 1960) when 'the Doctor'
(accompanied by Mrs. Lloyd-Jones) preached at Llanddewibrefi.
There were two sermons, both in Welsh, with about 900 people
present. This day was notable for Vernon in several ways. He

received some fatherly advice, shared various matters about the work of the ministry in a friendly and intimate way, but that was not all. At the end of the evening meeting MLl-J insisted that Vernon should accept the day's preaching fee as a gift.

MLl-J preached regularly at Heath — in fact, he did so for fifty-four years altogether, making his final visit there in October 1979. On such occasions he would usually stay with Vernon for lunch and tea. He was also a source of immense encouragement when separation from the Presbyterian Church of Wales was being negotiated between 1970 and 1976. For Vernon this was obviously a lonely and anxious time, and he greatly valued discussing the many issues with MLl-J on the telephone, and also when the two men and their wives met in London, or in Cardiff when he was being interviewed by the B.B.C. Initial friendship had by now deepened considerably into something lasting and strong. In a sense Vernon had become a part of the Lloyd-Jones family scene.

Vernon also mentioned a number of other incidents which were connected with his own ill health (caused by asthma and related problems). One Saturday in 1965 he was so weak that he felt unable to carry on with his ministry. On hearing this 'the Doctor', who was due to travel to Swansea by train, altered his schedule and instead drove to Cardiff to visit Vernon in his home where he urged him to go on with the work of preaching. Another incident occurred the day before MLl-J's annual visit to Heath in 1972. The consultant had decided that Vernon would have to remain in hospital, thus causing him to miss what he regarded as the highlight of his year. Again MLl-J visited him in hospital and also talked briefly with the other patients there. After he had left to fulfil his preaching engagement, one of them turned to Vernon and asked who the visitor had been. At first he gave a non-committal reply, and asked why the man wanted to know. The answer was: 'Because he (MLl-J) was so clean.' A little later, Vernon was walking round the ward when he encountered a man who suffered a great deal from asthma. He was a very sick man, but he said this: 'We asthma sufferers are experts on the dawn; we often wait for it, but now I would say that the mirage has become a pool, and the dawn has become the dawn of belief.'

Here was another man who had been converted as the result of MLl-J's ministry, this time through reading *The Mirage shall become a Pool*, which had been published in the period between 1947-49.

Vernon's final recollection concerned the meetings at the opening in 1977 of the Revd. Graham Harrison's church in Newport. He felt at a very low ebb, with a spirit of fear besetting him, so much so that MLl-J asked him, 'What's wrong?' He then suggested that they should pray together and resist Satan. Vernon felt God's presence in an intensely powerful way as they prayed. Not only was Satan resisted, but thereafter Vernon's asthmatic problems were healed; and he has not required medication since. Whereas previously he would not think of going away preaching at the weekend without a massive supply of drugs, he now goes away without even thinking of medicine.

Vernon's friendship with 'the Doctor' went on, as already indicated, right to the end. On his final visit to Ealing, MLl-J asked Vernon to remember two things: 'I'm only a sinner saved by grace, and please pray for an abundant entry into that everlasting kingdom.' Subsequently Vernon was asked to conduct MLl-J's funeral, and considered it a great honour to do so.

When asked what 'the Doctor' had meant to him, this is what Vernon said:

> He was totally genuine and could be trusted completely. You could tell him anything and feel absolutely sure it would be neither belittled nor despised. This integrity, this capacity for strengthening and comforting others, was also possessed by his wife. What was so pleasing about him was his kindly, teasing but never frivolous humour.
>
> As a preacher and minister, almost everything I knew I learnt from him. To hear him expounding the Word of God was one of life's greatest pleasures. He was a Christian gentleman whose career had a profound effect not only on ministers like myself, but also on ordinary people who flocked to hear him in such huge numbers.

4

Naturally there were those who had mixed views of 'the Doctor'. One is the *Revd. Charles Martin*. In a letter to me he outlined his situation like this:

> I came into the ministry of the Congregational Church in July 1972, just before the union with the Presbyterians. Until 1978 I remained undecided as to the future, but after that I made up my mind to remain within what was then the United Reformed Church. During my time of indecision I was a member of the Westminster Fellowship, and 'the Doctor' wrote two letters to me.
>
> The first was a very gracious and helpful reply to a letter I had written asking for advice. He read a little more into what I said that I had intended, and not only urged me to leave the U.R.C., but took it for granted that the decision had been made, and even offered help in finding a pastorate. Some time later I asked him to preach at the Silver Jubilee of the church I then served − St. George's Hampstead − in November 1979. He accepted, although we were all aware of the frailty of his health, but then withdrew his acceptance when he discovered that I had left the Westminster Fellowship because I had decided to remain a minister of the U.R.C. indefinitely. His second letter was courteous but clear in its severance of contact.

Charles Martin had definite opinions about MLl-J's impact on his denomination:

> My contact with him was late in the day, and most of the men he had affected had left the Congregational Union (later the Congregational Church) long before. However, I think his main impact was to challenge those of us who claimed to be evangelicals to take a stand for the Truth. In fact, he had two other effects: first, he polarized our denominations, or helped to do so: he made evangelicals into a fighting force; secondly, he encouraged some of us,

me included, to examine our motives were deeply, to sort out what we really felt about being an evangelical in today's world with its alien environment, and 'to run with perseverance the race set before us, looking unto Jesus'.

One thing that helped me make up my mind, and which I think he could never see, was that blemishes and defects exist in the Body of Christ wherever it is. Just because you claim to be a minister of the Evangelical Fellowship or Congregational Churches, or whatever grouping you choose, does not mean that you have escaped problems in the church. You may escape doctrinal impurity but may be just as riddled with pride and hard-heartedness, which must grieve the Holy Spirit just as much as doctrinal error, and which is just as much an offence to the gospel. I think it comes down to this: clarity of vision, which 'the Doctor' had in full measure, can sometimes obcure the more subtle but just as important considerations in the Christian faith and ministry. And the Holy Spirit is at work in places of which we seldom dream.

Charles Martin's viewpoint is not hostile. It is quite simply typical of many U.R.C. men's reactions in the years after MLl-J's October 1966 call. In fact, he says some generous positive things about MLl-J. It is not difficult, however, to see why the two men went in divergent ways. The argument ('You may escape doctrinal impurity . . .') would not have impressed 'the Doctor' at all. He would have claimed (I think quite rightly) that doctrine, correctly understood and applied, safeguards the Christian from pride, arrogance, or any other defect or un-Christian conduct for that matter. MLl-J never saw doctrine in isolation or divorced from every-day living.

5

There were of course many people whose only contacts with MLl-J were intermittent and long-range, but who, nevertheless, can offer a personal viewpoint on his ministry and preaching, and on the total effect of his personality and influence. One person in this category is the *Revd. William McMillan*[2], of Erskine, Scotland.

He started his Christian life as a conservative evangelical, but later moved away somewhat from that position. He reminded me, in a letter, of the opinion of the late minister of St. George's, Troon — the Revd. Tom Allan — that MLl-J 'was possibly the greatest biblical expositor in the English language'. McMillan remembered one of his visits to Scotland in the very late fifties or early sixties, in connection with a major event run by the National Bible Society of Scotland:

> This event was a series of meetings lasting a week. The Doctor spoke at a lunch-time service in St. George's Troon. His theme was 'Being Married to Christ'. These sermons lasted about thirty-five minutes (from 1.10pm– 1.45pm), as they were for city workers. He found the time limit restricting and was less inspiring than usual. Later, though, during the week he spoke at some of the evening rallies and really came into his own.

Another visit to Scotland was notable for a sermon on Acts 24. This is how McMillan described it to me:

> The subject of the sermon was 'Paul before Felix and Drusilla'. The sermon lasted an hour, but it did not seem long. It began with a character-sketch of the three people involved — like characters listed in a play by Shakespeare — and then went on to Paul's discourse on goodness, self-control, and judgement. Finally it touched on the reasons for Felix's rejection of the gospel.
>
> It was a great exposition and an altogether powerful sermon.

McMillan's third recollection concerned a series of youth rallies in the late 1960s:

> St. George's Troon was packed to capacity, with about 1,200 people present. The sermon was on Psalm 8 and

related to the American astronauts' landing on the moon. This time the sermon lasted one hour and fifteen minutes, and revolved around three crucial questions: What do we learn about God from this psalm? What does it show us about man? And, what do we learn from it about Jesus? All in all it was a challenging evening.

These occasions led McMillan to form a distinctive overall assessment of 'the Doctor':

Though not a fundamentalist, I have a high regard for him. He showed a great courage and consistency throughout his ministry and was utterly faithful to his calling as a preacher. He never skimped his preparations for preaching. I have recently purchased some of the cassettes of his sermons and listened to them with much profit and appreciation. He was undoubtedly a great man of God and, like many others, I have been blessed by his ministry.

Though perhaps less comprehensive than some of the other case-histories in this chapter, William McMillan's comments are significant and fair-minded. In spite of the fact that he is not a fundamentalist, he found MLl-J's preaching both invigorating and uplifting. He found MLl-J to be a man of integrity and of great faithfulness to his calling as a preacher. Above all, he conceived of him as a 'man of God'. This latter emphasis is accepted absolutely, even by those who — for reasons of controversy — object to certain aspects of his theology; and it is valid to draw attention to it in the way McMillan does.

6

All the viewpoints so far have been from experts or professionals, either ministers or academics. *Malcolm and Mary Sinden*, now living in Crawley Down, West Sussex, fit into neither of these categories. They worshipped regularly at Westminster Chapel in the early 1950s, but also had a number of contacts with MLl-J after they had moved away from London and after he had retired from the chapel. They last saw him when he made his annual visit to the Cotswold Bible Witness Rally, Chipping Norton, in 1976.

They had been brought up in Christian homes and had been totally immersed in the evangelical biblical faith all their lives. They became convinced and dedicated Christians as the result of a gradual process during their upbringing, but their faith was severely tested when they left their sheltered home environments. For Malcolm this happened when he entered the Forces during the latter part of World War Two; for Mary, when she enrolled at a teachers' training college. 'The Doctor' came to mean something very special to them. In their own words:

> Our familiarity with the gospel, our firm adoption of the faith, almost without question; our built-in defence mechanism against anything which was not 'sound', or which was 'of the world', had left certain God-shaped blanks in our minds, if not our hearts. Despite the years of faithful teaching which we had heard, there was a hint of familiarity, a slight sense of 'we know it all'. We were not, however, really prepared and equipped to give an absolutely convincing reason for the Hope within us.
>
> *This is where MLl-J came in.* For years we had, perhaps, had a defensive state of mind. In fact, we can recall a headstone outside one of our churches bearing the inscription 'Set for the defence of the gospel'. *This defensive, almost apologetic attitude was changed by the logical preaching of MLl-J.* In Wales he was said to have turned back the tide of apostasy in the church. In England his was a stern and certain voice which relied on 'straight from the shoulder', no-punches-pulled preaching, to press home the message.
>
> There was no place for a supporting cast, be it music or testimonies or gimmicks, current topics, or funny stories to hold the attention (which were the norm for many of his contemporaries). It was simply powerful and authoritative preaching alone, apart from a few rousing hymns of the faith, which always fitted the message.

His preaching always sent us away each time wondering how anyone could for one moment doubt the truth and logic of the gospel. The Doctor never 'apologized' for the gospel. We remember him as a *supreme advocate for the truth* who at the outset of his sermon and possibly following a brief re-cap would utterly demolish the 'devil's case'. It would be done with analytical precision and yet be plain enough for anyone to understand. After the 'demolition job' one could truly say, 'You know it makes sense' — and that was before hearing the positive part of the sermon on the saving and keeping grace in the Power of the Holy Spirit.

In common with many others, Malcolm and Mary Sinden's dominating impression of his preaching was of its authority and power. They were also adamant about another misapprehension about his time at Westminster Chapel:

Westminster Chapel was *not* just a preaching centre for Sunday commuters. It did provide an opportunity for many, who as students and young business people found themselves near enough to Central London to avail themselves of his preaching, but it was also a *family* chapel.

The encouragement the Sindens received from MLl-J's ministry became a continuing factor in their Christian experience when they later moved away from London and became involved in the challenge of Christian work in Orpington, Bournemouth, and Binscombe in Surrey. Their viewpoint is particularly valuable because it is that of the 'person in the pew'.

7

The next viewpoint is by someone who had a variety of contacts with 'the Doctor' over a period of almost forty years, *Pastor Harold J. Rodwell*,[3] now living in retirement in Durham.

Harold had come into contact initially with him in novel and unusual circumstances:

While reading one of the Doctor's sermons in *The Christian Herald* dated 11 February 1943, I came across his opinion that one of the most difficult types for the presentation of the Gospel is the agricultural worker. Perhaps because they spend so much of their time in the open air . . . they tend to slumber in to not too well-ventilated churches. I knew this statement to be untrue, and I was so angry that I felt I would challenge him if ever I was to meet him. The opportunity to do so came in October 1943 when on holiday in Worthing. I went along to the Tabernacle and after the service asked the steward for an interview. In his friendly manner the Doctor soon put me at ease. I then went on to talk about the sermon I had read in *The Christian Herald* and said that if he would come to my church to preach, I would provide him with a congregation of farmers and their employees who would not go to sleep. The Doctor was so amused that he agreed to take up my challenge.

The upshot of this conversation was that MLl-J conducted the next Chapel Anniversary at Yelling, Huntingdonshire on 30 May 1944. The chapel was full for both afternoon and evening service. Thus began an acquaintance which lasted to the end of MLl-J's life. Indeed, one of the last letters he ever wrote (dated 4 December 1980) was sent to Harold Rodwell:

My dear Friend,
    How good it was to receive your most kind letter. It really brought me great joy.
    I remember all the facts and events to which you refer most vividly and thinking of these makes me thank God.
    Unfortunately I am not well. I have had two operations, one in 1976 and another this year in June. Since the latter I have been able to do no work and I have to go into hospital every 3-4 weeks which is rather weakening. But we both rejoice in the goodness of our gracious God and thank Him for all the long years He has given us and endless blessings.

I well understand how you feel — but God will guide you.

We all as a family join in sending our warm loving greetings to you all and our prayers that God may bless you more and more.

Yours sincerely,

D.M. Lloyd-Jones

'The Doctor' was undoubtedly a *private* person. To some he seemed dour, even cold and austere. For many, reading Murray's biography has left them frustrated at their inability to grasp what it was like to be in truly personal contact with him. Harold Rodwell's impressions therefore constitute an important contribution because they say a great deal about the man himself:

The Doctor had a wonderful way of putting me at ease. He never assumed himself to be greater than anyone else. He was always ready to listen and hear, and very slow to pass judgement.

I felt I could approach him on any subject, particularly in the early days of my marriage with regard to family planning. Our friendship became somewhat strained when I left the Baptist Church and joined the Church of England in 1950, and he was much happier when I was able to inform him that I was re-ordained in the Baptist Church in 1967.

No matter how big the crowd or how busy he was with other people, I always felt I could approach him for a few words of greeting and if possible a word of prayer. He was always interested in my wife and family, my church and my farm. Although I did not see him to speak to after we left East Anglia in 1970, we kept in touch by letter almost to the end.

I shall always remember him as one who walked with God. He had a great passion for souls and the well-being of the Church of the Living God, and loved to proclaim the doctrine of Free and Sovereign Grace.

Harold Rodwell's recollections show that MLl-J was a most approachable person. There is genuine warmth in his letters[4] to Rodwell, while Rodwell's comments illustrate clearly the combination of spirituality and humanity which made 'the Doctor' such a stable person, whose counsel was so wise and constructive. He had a sensitive touch in dealing with people. He was disciplined but not coldly austere, serious but also compassionate.

7

For a final viewpoint I approached *Professor G.N.M. Collins*, formerly of the Free College, Edinburgh. He is well-placed to comment on 'the Doctor', being an academic, a preacher, and his personal friend. In a long letter to me he recalled that MLl-J's name was familiar in Scotland long before he preached there.

But there were also reservations. Was it right, it was asked, that a man trained for such an important profession as medicine should turn from it, to enter another profession for which he had not trained? The Scots felt too that MLl-J was an eccentric — admittedly in the best sense of the term, but eccentrics had to be treated with caution. It was true that he had made a brilliant beginning, but would he stay the course? When, therefore, he was brought to Scotland for a series of week-night addresses in Glasgow, in 1938, crowded audiences took the opportunity of judging for themselves. The verdict was unanimous: 'A new voice for God was beginning to sound in the land, and men were listening. A new apostolic ministry had begun. Glasgow was convinced, but would the people of Edinburgh be equally convinced?

Their chance to assess 'the Doctor' came in April 1939, when he was invited to hold a week's mission in the Usher Hall in Edinburgh:

Night after night the great Hall was filled with eager hearers — young people prominent among them. The techniques of modern evangelism were nowhere in evidence.

The preaching was plain, solid, searching and arresting. Edinburgh was of one mind with Glasgow regarding this man and his message,. and by those early meetings, Dr. Lloyd-Jones won a place in the hearts of Scottish evangelicals that he retained for the rest of his life. More requests for service reached him than he could ever hope to accept; the wonder was that he accepted so many. The Scottish Evangelical Council brought him back again and again to address meetings arranged for him in the largest Halls in Glasgow, Edinburgh, Dundee and Aberdeen. Inverness claimed him, and so did Dingwall and Stornoway, until his name became a household word even in the remoter areas of the country.

This visit took place at a particularly significant time in the religious life of Scotland:

Scotland had already had its Forward Movement, its Recall to Religion Campaign, its Sword of the Spirit testimony, and had resorted to various other expedients with a view to producing a more exhilarating spiritual climate; but the results were disappointing. The Church was still in the doldrums, and seemed destined to remain there. The ecumenical leaders were busy with their blue-prints for the coming 'World Church', but things were not proceeding according to plan. . . .

Yet, as in the days of Jeremiah, when men in their perplexity cried, 'Is there any word from the Lord?', the reply again came, 'There is.' It was not a new one, but it was fully contemporary and totally relevant, as the Word of God always is.

Collins referred to MLl-J's unique style of answering questions:

At a meeting for ministers arranged for him in Inverness on one occasion, Dr. Lloyd-Jones was asked if he would pin-point any signs of promise that he saw in the Church situation as he travelled around. This he did, carefully adducing and analysing events and situations which appeared to hold out promise of good things to come.

In the discussion that ensued, one minister expressed surprise that, among the promising things which were currently happening, the Doctor had not even mentioned the Ecumenical movement. Would he explain why?

The explanation was immediately forthcoming. He had not mentioned the Ecumenical movement because he regarded it as entirely irrelevant!

But his questioner was not satisfied. Surely, he persisted, it must be regarded as of the utmost promise that a large number of Churches were being brought together in the interests of Christian unity. What clearer omen of coming revival could be sought?

'Do you really believe, then,' came the reply, 'that if you take a number of isolated dead bodies and lay them out side by side, they will come alive? It is an interesting theory, but I'm afraid I cannot accept it.'

The discomfited questioner gave up!

On this incident Collins makes the following comment:

The answer, however, was not given in naughty facetious-ness. In the Doctor's judgment, the enterprises of Liberal ecumenism could never achieve their avowed purpose. The Spirit of Truth would not acknowledge an effort that was so obviously at variance with the ultimate standards of revealed Truth.

He also pin-pointed several reasons for the warmth of MLl-J's reception amongst the Scottish evangelicals; including this one:

. . . his ready willingness to become associated with the work of minority groups and denominations who were endeavouring to maintain a clear-cut Reformed witness, sometimes in extremely difficult circumstances. He indeed became a living link between several of these bodies and we looked to him for all our special occasions.

Finally, this is how Collins summed up his overall impression of 'the Doctor':

> We all seemed, tacitly, to acknowledge Dr. Lloyd-Jones' leadership in ecumenical matters. We formed the British Evangelical Council after discussions in Edinburgh, and planned it on interdenominational lines by electing founder-members from England, Scotland, Wales and Ireland. The Doctor, all through, was helpful, and the growth of the Council over the years owed much to his wise guidance.
>
> Dr. Lloyd-Jones was indeed 'a great man given to the Church in a time of need', and while he will be remembered especially for his work in England and Wales, where his two pastoral charges were situated, Scotland has good reason to pay its own tribute to his memory. His converts are to be found throughout our borders, even to the remotest islands around our shores. News of his death stunned us although we were aware that recovery from his illness was not expected. But while we mourned the passing of a leader we could ill spare, we rejoiced together in his rich and ongoing ministry, for truly, 'he being dead yet speaketh.'

These case histories are important for a number of reasons, not least for their range. Where they diverge they are as valuable as their points of agreement, and they are significant in building up a composite picture of the man and his ministry. Consider the spread and variety involved. Moon is an avowedly evangelical minister who was converted as a result of MLl-J's preaching. Connell is an academic who spent most of his career in a conservative Bible College, and who found some of MLl-J's theology unacceptable. Higham represents the Welsh and Reformed branches of the evangelical world, with an extremely high view of the importance of preaching and the role of the

minister. Martin is representative of opinion within the United
Reformed Church which opposed the October 1966 call for the
formation of a new evangelical grouping. McMillan gives a long-
range and non-evangelical view of his ministry. The Sindens sat
regularly under the ministry of 'the Doctor' at Westminster
Chapel, and found something in it of permanent and lasting
value. Rodwell had a personal link with him over many years,
while Collins was a friend, a minister, and an acute observer
of the evangelical world, both in Scotland and England.
Differences of temperament, culture, education, and ecclesiology
exist between these people, but they are at one in their insistence
on MLl-J's powerfully instructive ministry, and his willingness
to help with a host of spiritual, emotional, and other problems,
his integrity as a man of God, and his devotion to his family.
They confirm that his influence was beneficial, frequently
radical, and always strengthening. Each in his own way pointed
to the unity and reality of his life, as a man and as a minister.
These views are a paradigm of the significance of his life and
ministry.

CHAPTER 6

Some Reflections

In this chapter we shall bring together and assess some of the salient features of the man and his work.

THE MAN

He had immense intellectual powers. His academic success at Bart's came as no surprise to his family or to those of his associates who knew him well. As a physician he was able to diagnose skilfully and comprehensively, a capacity which was early recognized by Horder. It is likely that had he continued in medicine he would have become both eminent and wealthy. Naturally the fact that he was leaving medicine aroused much media interest when he left London for the grimly depressed areas of Aberavon in South Wales.

This attention was not something he welcomed then or subsequently, for he was essentially a *private* person who consistently drew a discreet but firm veil over his activities outside Westminster Chapel. He prevented the publication of at least two biographies, and he refused, on a number of other occasions, to sanction accounts of his life. I know this to be true from personal experience. In 1975, I wrote to him asking for permission to include him in a projected book on 'Men of God'. His reply, though courteous, was quite definite in its refusal:

                                                    September 5th, 1975.

Dear Mr Peters,
    Many thanks for your letter which was forwarded to me from home (he was staying in Cambridge with his daughter Elizabeth and her husband Fred (Sir Frederick Catherwood)). I have considered this matter on previous occasions when similar suggestions have been put to me and have always felt that no really useful purpose could be served by it. However, having received your letter I have thought about it again, but still find myself of the same opinion.
    It was good of you to have thought of including me and I appreciate the honour you do me.
    With all good wishes,
    Yours sincerely,
    D.M. Lloyd-Jones

His opposition to and dislike of any parade of self was maintained throughout his life. He did though co-operate, towards the end of his life, with the Revd. Iain Murray, who had begun to prepare a biography with the full backing of the Lloyd-Jones family, especially Mrs. Lloyd-Jones. I stress this because one review of Murray's first volume, by Michael Harper, headed 'Elusive Doctor', commented as follows:

> MLl-J must have been almost the only man of any significance who avoided the media's attention so successfully. He gave only one interview during his entire life and his only TV appearances were on Welsh language programmes

and then added:

> He was not exactly helpful to any potential biographer and

Iain Murray has done the best he could with limited resources.

The reality is, of course, that an overwhelmingly large part of the volume referred to was prepared, in Murray's own words, 'in consultation with him, and that the general interpretation which it gives of his career is his own'. MLl-J's direct involvement continued from 1980 almost until his death.

MLl-J was a man with many interests outside preaching, theology and medicine. He was passionately interested, for example, in music, and took a keen interest in politics — though he never preached on political themes — and cricket. Pressure of work prevented him from attending many matches, but Mrs. Lloyd-Jones told me that for a number of years he greatly enjoyed his yearly visit to the Test Match at Lord's.

He was a devoted family man. This was impressed upon Dr. R.T. Kendall one evening as MLl-J and his wife were putting on their coats after a meal at the manse:

> (His) eyes moistened as he looked at me and said: 'There is only one thing in life I ever really wanted. I never really wanted to excel in medicine or in anything else. There is only one thing that ever gripped me to the point that I would have done anything to achieve it.' 'What on earth was that?' I asked. He just looked at his wife. He regarded winning her as his life's companion as the greatest thing that ever happened to him other than becoming a Christian. Such affection was extended to his two daughters and grandchildren. He loved Elizabeth and Ann with an affection that most children never know. His only hesitation in going to glory was leaving his wife and family behind.[1]

Undoubtedly the security and stability of his family was a source of great comfort to him throughout his life. At this point it is only right and appropriate to say something about Mrs. Lloyd-Jones. She was a highly qualified doctor herself, but when I asked her how she saw her role in relation to her husband's

preaching and ministry, she said: 'To keep him happy and in
the pulpit'. This remarkably modest statement obscures the fact
that theirs was a team effort in the fullest meaning of that word.

The significance of all this can be demonstrated by referring
to a remark 'the Doctor' made in the ambulance taking him to
hospital for a serious operation in March 1968. After indicating
to Mrs. Lloyd-Jones his belief that his ministry at Westminster
Chapel ought to be drawn to a close, he said: 'It's the end for
you too.' She had been a natural and wise go-between (for both
minister and congregation) for thirty years, and she was
frequently consulted on pastoral matters at the chapel. It is hardly
surprising, therefore, that members were as shattered by her
departure as by his. Such was the esteem and respect with which
people viewed her contribution to the chapel's life and worship.
Here again we can refer to some words Dr. Kendall wrote in
the Memorial Number of the *Westminster Record* (June 1981):
'I am certain that Heaven will reveal that Dr. Lloyd-Jones's
success had a lot to do with his wife'. Few would wish to dissent
from this verdict.

Thus the change was not without its deep personal effect on
Mrs. Lloyd-Jones for whom the chapel had been, in her own
words, 'her life'. She continued to attend Westminster Chapel
after her husband's retirement, being careful to enter after the
first hymn and to leave before the last one. This arrangement
was largely at the insistence of MLl-J who, above all, did not
wish his successor to feel that the previous minister's family was
looking over his shoulder.

As a person, 'the Doctor' was essentially serious-minded,
never frivolous, though with a finely developed sense of humour.
He was also a man of disciplined and voracious reading habits.
A glimpse of this is given in *Preaching and Preachers*, where
he says that in the early days of his ministry he regarded reading
through the entire Bible in a year as the very 'minimum'[2] for
a minister. This process of continuous and applied reading went
on in the holidays too. As with everything else he did, his reading
was balanced, and his advice to the students at Westminster
Theological Seminary — he gave a series of lectures there in
1969 — was that they should read not only theology but also

biographies, church history (especially revivals), and the more devotional type of reading.

MLl-J was a Welsh-speaking Welshman. He was thoroughly conversant with the history, literature and culture of Wales, and at home he spoke only Welsh to his wife. This aspect of his life was given prominence in one of the obituaries published in the Welsh language. The newspaper, *Y Faner*, laid great stress on his 'Welshness', stating that 'a theology of the nation was part of the Faith to him', adding: 'He loved Wales as a country. Her land was important to him and he came to visit and enjoy it' (my translation).

THE CHRISTIAN

'The Doctor' was a man of God. His own testimony, 'Why I am a Christian',[3] concentrates on the activity of God the Father, Son and Holy Spirit in his life:

> I am a Christian solely and entirely because of the grace of God and not because of anything that I have thought or said or done.

> It was He who by His Holy Spirit quickened me and awakened me to the realization of certain profound and vital truths taught in the Bible.

> He brought me to know that I was 'dead in trespasses and sins', a slave to the world, and the flesh, and the devil, that in me 'dwelleth no good thing', and that I was under the wrath of God and heading for eternal punishment.

> He brought me to see that the real cause of all my troubles and ills, and that of all men, was an evil and fallen nature which hated God and loved sin. My trouble was not only that I did things that were wrong but that I myself was wrong at the very centre of my being.

> This led me to the realization that I was helpless as well as hopeless, for 'Can the Ethiopian change his skin, or the leopard his spots?' All moral teaching and moral effort

were useless for God demands perfection. I could not atone for my past sins, and I could not please God in the present, or hope to do so in the future.

Then He revealed to me the Lord Jesus Christ as the Son of God who had come into the world 'to seek and to save that which is lost'. He taught me that Christ had died for my sins — bearing my punishment in His death upon the Cross — and that He had also rendered a perfect obedience to God's laws on my behalf. As a result of this God forgave me freely, and in addition imputed the righteousness of His Son to me, regarding me as if I had never sinned at all. Moreover, He created in me a new nature and made me a new man. He adopted me into His family as one of His sons, and showed me that I was a joint heir with Christ of a glorious inheritance in heaven.

'By the grace of God I am what I am'
'Soli Deo Gloria'

He was a man of God in that he followed Paul's advice to flee from such things as love of money, to follow after righteousness, faith, love, meekness, and the rest, and to fight the fight of faith (1 Tim. 6:11-12).

He was a man of God in another sense too: in the major events of his life he was conscious of divine guidance and leading. Indeed he saw his whole life as being *solely and entirely governed by the operation of God's grace*, a fact which gave him his authenticity as a preacher. God's hand was nowhere more in evidence than in the closing months of his life. This period was characterized by peaceful acceptance and tranquillity, proving eloquently what he had taught over the years: that a sure test of a person's Christian profession is the manner in which the crises of life are faced, especially death. Mrs. Lloyd-Jones told me that during the last week of his life MLl-J was unable to speak very much and instead wrote notes to his family on a small paper pad. One to his daughter, Ann, who was naturally looking distressed and worried, read: 'Don't be anxious or worried — Philippians 4:6-7.'[4] Another, this time to his wife, said: 'Contact the paper shop and cancel Times permanently from Saturday.' A third is even more significant: 'Don't pray for my healing. Don't try to hold me back from the glory.' MLl-J was not without his critics, but none would deny that he was in the fullest sense a man of God.

THE EVANGELICAL LEADER

Clearly he was one of the twentieth century's foremost evangelical leaders. Some of the highlights are worth recording: his courageous work during the horrifying and dismal years of the Second World War when the Free Churches were under an intolerable strain; the rebuilding of the congregation at Westminster Chapel a long expository lines; the publication, at his insistence, of such volumes as Bishop Ryle's *Holiness*; his tremendous contribution to the growth in general of the U.C.C.A. (formerly I.V.F.), and also his role in the Biblical Research Committee of that movement; his part in the Puritan Conference; his chairmanship of the Westminster Fellowship; his support for the Evangelical Library[5] which now has branches in many countries, including Africa, North and South America, and Australasia; his encouragement to the Banner of Truth Trust, and his positive and biblical response to the insistent clamour of the Ecumenical Movement. These are but a few of the many ways in which he influenced and encouraged evangelicals in a career spanning over fifty years.

I asked the Revd. Vernon Higham what he meant to the evangelical life of Wales. He replied: 'Without the work and influence of Dr. Lloyd-Jones there would not have been an evangelical life in Wales, and his inspiration to the Evangelical Movement of Wales and the annual conference of evangelical ministers was immense'. Much the same could be said of his influence on the evangelical life of England.

How instructive and enlightening it would have been, had MLl-J written himself about these and other related matters! In this respect he was highly paradoxical, because he constantly persuaded others to publish their works, whereas he himself was into his sixties before he brought out a major volume of his own. Few perhaps will be aware that it was largely due to his influence that Professor Keri Evans's autobiography was published, in Welsh in the first instance, and that, twenty years later, a translation into English appeared as *My Spiritual Pilgrimage: From Philosophy to Faith.*

THE PREACHER

We have already considered in chapter 3 the dominating characteristics of MLl-J's preaching. But great preachers are valued by individuals for a variety of personal reasons. The following pages are an attempt to outline what I personally valued in his preaching.

First, there was his *preoccupation with the glory of God.* This was a recurring theme in his sermons. He taught that to be occupied with God's glory is to lift our minds, hearts, bodies and personalities above the mortal and the finite and to fix them on that timeless and infinite realm where God reigns supreme.

Such a preoccupation was also notable in his prayers.[6] Whenever I attended his services, whether at Westminster Chapel, or in Wales, or in Surrey, I felt uplifted and strengthened as he invited his congregation to gaze and to worship the One installed permanently 'in glory'. God's person and incomparable glory was always the starting-point for him. In his minute analyses of theological problems and often intricate passages he would begin with what is firmly established (God's character), proceeding then to the diagnosis and the solution, always in terms of God's glorious and authoritative Word. For me, MLl-J portrayed the essential glory of God as something stupendous, awe-inspiring, magnificent; something of unmatchable majesty.

Secondly, there was his *insistence on the wonder of the gospel.* Fundamental to his character was this state of being enraptured, exhilarated, and enthralled by the gospel; it was a thrill he never lost. On his first visit to Sandfields on 28 November 1926 he spoke on 1 Corinthians 2:2 ('Jesus Christ and him crucified'), and on the fiftieth anniversary of the commencement of his ministry in Aberavon he returned there to preach on the same text. In the course of his opening remarks on this occasion (in February 1977), he said that this sublime text was 'an expression' of his 'whole attitude to life'.

To 'the Doctor' the gospel was the *only* solution to man's desperate plight, his lostness, his depravity in sin. Like Paul he was proud of the gospel because it is God's way of Salvation, because it works, and because it works for everyone. This is how he conceived of the appeal and worth of the gospel:

> No, the glory of the Gospel is that it is primarily an announcement of what God does, and has done, in the Person of Jesus Christ. That was the essence of Paul's Gospel, as he proceeds to show in the remainder of the Epistle. That was the Gospel which was preached by all the Apostles. They preached Jesus as the Christ. They made a proclamation, an announcement. Primarily, they called upon people to listen to what they called 'good news'. They did not in the first instance outline a programme for life and living. They were not setters forth of a point of view which they called upon people to accept. They did not go round the world in the first instance propagating a new order or a new scheme for living. They began by stating facts and explaining what they meant. They preached, not a programme, but a Person. They said that Jesus of Nazareth was the Son of God come from Heaven to earth. They said that He manifested and demonstrated His unique deity by living a perfect, spotless, sinless life of complete obedience to God, and by performing miracles. His death on the Cross was not merely the end of His life but the result of His rejection by His own countrymen, it had a deeper and more eternal significance. It was something that had to happen in order that mankind might be reconciled to God. It was a transaction between God the Father and God the Son. It was the Son bearing our sins 'in His own body on the tree,' and the fulfilment of the ancient prophecy of Isaiah, who had said that the Messiah would be 'bruised for our transgressions,' and that

'by his stripes we shall be healed.' Indeed, as Paul put it
elsewhere, 'God was in Christ reconciling the world unto
himself' and making 'him to be sin for us, who knew no
sin; that we might be made the righteousness of God in
him' (2 Corinthians 5.21). But that was not all. He had
risen from the grave, had manifested Himself unto certain
chosen witnesses, and then ascended into Heaven. From
Heaven He had sent the gift of the Holy Spirit upon the
early Church, and He had brought unto them not only new
understanding, but new life and power. Their lives had
been entirely changed, and they now had life which was
life indeed. That was the message. Its entire emphasis was
upon what God had done. Its content was God's way of
salvation and of making men righteous. Man had but to
accept it and submit to it.[7]

Thirdly, we may single out from this passage a characteristic
that he shared with the apostles: an *emphasis on the facts*. He
insisted, and consistently demonstrated, that without the whole
Bible it is impossible to 'understand the truth in its fullness'.
This is largely self-explanatory, and is a frequent theme in his
preaching.[8]

Lastly, there was *the whole question of spiritual thinking*. A
number of the obituaries published after his death in March 1981
made reference to the fact that he taught many ministers to think,
and then to think spiritually. He did not offer pious platitudes,
impractical cliches, emotional escapism, or an easy pragmatism.
Instead, from his deep knowledge of the Scriptures and of life,
he brought an honest and realistic mind to bear upon life in all
its complexity. This is particularly noticeable in his book *Faith
on Trial*. He takes the problems of the man in Psalm 73 — why
the godly suffer while the ungodly appear to be most prosperous
— and places it over against several important principles: that
God is always good to his people, that to be tempted and to be
perplexed is not sinful, that we must know how to handle
temptation when it comes, that one of the enriching and
indispensable qualities of the Christian life is discipline, and that
whatever the problem is it must never be faced or approached

in isolation from the rest of God's truth.

In a subsequent chapter on 'The Importance of Spiritual Thinking', he shows the great need for spiritual thinking on *all* aspects of the Christian life (not merely *rational* thinking). He also shows that Christians are to promote and encourage spiritual thinking by frequenting the house of God, by reading God's Word, and by praying and meditating. His advice on the last point needs to be noted carefully: 'Before we can truly pray we must think spiritually. There is nothing more fatuous than glib talk about prayer, as if prayer were something which you can always immediately rush into!' Here is sound, sensible (but perhaps not popular) advice.

But as he often claimed himself, preaching must be related to a definite pastoral concern, and this was precisely the impression conveyed to a visitor to Westminster Chapel in the last year of MLl-J's ministry there:

> I can remember Dr Lloyd-Jones preaching on Romans when I visited Westminster Chapel (I am an Anglican) as a student. I was not so much impressed by the exposition (by now I was used to University Christian Union speakers) but by the way in which his sermon became a pastoral occasion. Here was not just straight exposition but a word to the heart in a receptive atmosphere — surely brought about by many years of praying over the scriptures.
>
> What was impressed upon me when I visited Westminster Chapel in 1968 was that a work of prayer and faithful pastoring had brought together a fellowship that was hungry for God's word. In this I think Lloyd-Jones made his impact on the church by holding forth such a fruitful ministry.[9]

The last sentence here is the key to the emotional quality and effect of his career, and it may well be that his *greatest* influence was through his pulpit and pastoral ministry. For as people all over the world read his sermons or listen to him on cassette, they would remember that small, soberly dressed figure peering out at his congregation. He would certainly have echoed the famous statement of Jan Huss:

> By the help of God I have preached, still am preaching,
> and if His grace will allow, shall continue to preach; if
> perchance I may be able to lead some poor, tired, or halting
> soul into the house of Christ to the King's supper.[10]

THE LEGACY

It is now over five years since 'the Doctor' died at his West
London home. Murray's first volume established a secure
biographical base for the years 1899–1939, and Volume Two
will complete the project.

The stage is therefore set for a balanced assessment of his
ministry and influence : a sort of critical consensus. Indeed,
the Revd. Donald Macleod has already begun the process by
considering the nature and extent of 'The Lloyd-Jones Legacy'
in *The Monthly Record of the Free Church of Scotland*
(December 1983). This was the title he gave to his review of
Murray's first volume. In it he says a number of generous things,
including this crisp opinion:

> It was not simply that in an age of pygmies he towered
> above the others. Indeed he was arguably the greatest
> preacher since the Reformation, rivalled only by
> Whitefield, Spurgeon and Chalmers.

He observes that 'the Doctor' bestrode English and Welsh
evangelicalism like a colossus and his death was a traumatic event
for the whole movement'. On the other hand, Macleod draws
attention, in considerable detail, to what he considers to be
'problem' areas in MLl-J's ministry.

First, the precise nature of his call, about which he comments:

> It was the Doctor's personal decision to enter the ministry.
> It was also his personal decision not to train according
> to the normal course prescribed by his denomination and

not to enter its regular ministry. Finally, it was his personal decision to begin his work at Sandfields. In all this individualism he was typical of generations of evangelicals, including ourself.

A little later in his article he says this:

The idea that the call to the ministry is mainly inward has a long pedigree. Theologically, however, the most that can be said for it is that there is indeed an inward constraint that leads a man to aspire to the work of the eldership (1 Tim. 3:1). In today's terms that means a desire to offer oneself as a candidate for the ministry. But that is all the inward call creates. It creates *candidates*, not ministers. Only the external call of an authentic church creates a minister.

Secondly, Macleod refers to the whole question of ministerial training, something which 'the Doctor' had not of course undergone, and observes:

Many have taken courage from the Doctor's example to argue against the need for ministers to be trained. But the argument is ill-considered. Whatever his attitude to theological colleges Dr Lloyd-Jones had had the advantage of a rigorous university education. He had also received a thorough professional training as a medical clinician. Beyond that, certainly, he taught himself. But that does not mean that any young man fresh from school, office or factory can do the same. To be perfectly logical, what the Doctor's career proves is that every preacher must have an outstanding intellect, a distinguished university career and a brilliant professional reputation.

Thirdly, the 'Doctor cult', upon which he offers this judgement:

In a quite unique way he functioned as the Cardinal Archbishop of evangelicalism, participating in the

Westminster Fellowship, the Westminster Conference, the British Evangelical Council and the Evangelical Movement of Wales not as an ordinary minister but as a different order of being. As a matter of course, he was always given prime time and special deference, no matter who else was present. This was not something he sought. It was thrust upon him. But he was wrong to accept it.

Macleod's strictures must be taken seriously. The first of them may be contrasted with MLl-J's own conception of his call to the ministry:

> Whatever authority I am may have as a preacher is not the result of any decision on my part. It was God's hand that laid hold on me, and drew me out, and separated me to this work. I am what I am because of God's grace; and I give Him all the glory.[11]

There is no compelling reason to doubt this version of the events, and it is worth recalling that the London Presbytery approved of 'the Doctor' as a candidate for the ministry.

The second criticism ignores a fundamental biblical principle: that the divine call is attended by the divine equipping for service.

Thirdly, the question of the so-called 'Doctor cult'. The choice of the word 'cult' is perhaps unfortunate, but it is undeniable that MLl-J did occupy an 'unique' position within evangelicalism. This was something that gradually evolved, especially after the move to Westminster Chapel. It was a totally spontaneous process, a response, no less, to what was perfectly obvious to impartial and objective observers: that MLl-J was an authoritative figure of outstanding and rare quality. What is altogether less clear is Macleod's suggestion as to how 'the Doctor' ought to have behaved:

> He should have borne testimony by his example to the parity of ministers. He should have given others an oppor- tunity to develop their gifts of leadership (for example, by chairing the Westminster Fellowship). He should have

taken positive steps to minimise evangelicalism's dependence on himself. That he did none of these things was probably (and paradoxically) a reflection of his own shyness. He may have found it easier to go along with men's wishes than to contradict them.

MLl-J's individualism and strength of character was such that it is difficult to see how men, in Macleod's opinion, forced on Dr. Lloyd-Jones a wrong style of leadership. He was not the sort of man to have anything forced on him. What really happened was that he emerged as a natural leader by virtue of his preaching, his undoubted spiritual qualities, and his fearlessness in expounding and defending historic Christianity. Professor Collins put it succinctly: 'We all seemed, tacitly, to acknowledge Dr. Lloyd-Jones's leadership in ecumenical matters.'[12] Donald Macleod's distinctly iconoclastic review, has, however, performed the useful purpose of causing people to think carefully and seriously about the legacy bequeathed to us. An appraisal of this issue must evaluate at least two factors, one personal, the other written.

The first of them is the *collective memory* of those who heard him preach, or who were counselled by him, or who were influenced by his theological opinions and assertions in a more general way. Not untypical of this collective memory is the following tribute by the Revd. Donald Elcoat, Rector of St. Aidan's, Hull:

I first heard 'the Doctor' preach at Westminster Chapel on the first Sunday morning, if my memory serves me, of 8th November 1957. I cannot remember either the text — except that it was from Ephesians — or what was said, but I know that I was moved to open tears. Although I had been a Christian for five years, I felt that I had been converted all over again. I had heard many fine addresses as a member of my university Christian Union, but none had moved me as much as the Doctor's.

Gradually, during the year I spent working at the offices of the Banner of Truth, I grew in knowledge of the

Christian faith and, I trust, in the Christian graces which
the Doctor was at pains to stress were the outward signs
of a true profession. I had opportunities to meet him
personally but I was too shy avail myself of many of them,
though I longed to do so, since I had heard of many others
being helped by his regular surgeries.

Several years later, in 1966, having attended the 80th
Anniversary of the International Miners' Mission the
previous day, I delayed my return to the north east in order
to attend the morning service at Westminster Chapel. I
asked the Steward to obtain an interview for me with the
Doctor.

I was ushered into the vestry. His back was towards me
as he supped a well-earned cup of tea. I stood in silence,
not wishing to disturb him. At length I cleared my throat.
He turned on seeing me and was full of apologies. On
explaining the reason for my visit to London, I discovered
that he knew more of the history of the mission than I did:
it had started life in South Wales as the Glynn Vivian
Miners' Mission. I do not know whether it was any of his
doing, but the next A.G.M. was held at Westminster
Chapel.

I thank God for the life and teaching of Dr. Lloyd-
Jones.[13]

His ministry was equally beneficial to perfectly ordinary
members of his regular (and occasional) congregations, as this
completely unpretentious and delightfully honest extract from
a letter to me confirms:

I don't know much about the life of Dr Lloyd-Jones, but
I remember one Sunday morning many years ago when
my husband asked where we were going to worship that
day. We were Pentecostals, and it was difficult to be
satisfied. At once I said, 'Oh, Dr Lloyd-Jones — he has
got something.' We went to his church till we moved away
and were always satisfied.[14]

In some cases, as with John Davies of Warwickshire, memories extend back well over fifty years:

> My Father knew the Doctor and he called at our home in Gorseinon, near Swansea more than once. This was when Dr Lloyd-Jones was minister at Sandfields, Aberavon. I was myself privileged to hear him preach many times in Welsh, and the last time at Tumble (near Carmarthen) on the text 'Be ye therefore perfect'. After his retirement I heard him preach in English at a crowded evangelical church in Swansea.[15]

For some, however, his memory is tinged with controversy, even acrimony. This was primarily to do with his call in 1966 for evangelicals to join together. One person I corresponded with — who was otherwise tremendously impressed with his preaching — had this to say:

> As an Anglican I was disappointed with his 'come out from among them' sermon. The context of this I believe was holiness. In my view there is no warrant for evangelical christians to leave historic denominations, rather to work for renewal and reformation from within. My belief is that such a message was wrong, and while there is a reformation basis within the mainline traditions, then there is much scope for work and fellowship.[16]

A more extreme reaction to the same meeting was sent to me by someone who knew I was working on this book. It said this:

> John Stott, deeply hurt by his caricature of evangelical Anglicans' alleged ecclesiology of 'the fishing pool' strategy, handled the atmosphere with dignity and incontrovertible logic.
> My mind boggled at the irony of this preacher seeking to be a rallying call for all Evangelicals leaving their churches when he was clearly out of sympathy with evangelism, Deepening of the Spiritual Life conferences,

prophecy, as accepted by most of them. I also knew from friends at the London Bible College that Dr Lloyd-Jones was the odd man out there on apologetics, Bible introduction, historical theology.

When I came home to London in 1977 when both Stott and Lloyd-Jones had retired from the ministry of their city churches, it became clear that the former had built an ecclesia, with lay training and local outreach, whereas Westminster Chapel was down to less than two hundred: the latter had had an audience but not an ecclesia.[17]

While these comments verge at times on the acerbic, they do represent opinions (primarily amongst Anglicans) which cannot be ignored in any balanced assessment of MLl-J's life. One or two of the points call for particular attention. The first, regarding Stott's handling of that admittedly difficult meeting, is at best a matter of personal opinion. Many people I spoke to gave a radically different version to the one quoted above. The second criticism is altogether too sweeping and inaccurate. To claim that 'the Doctor' was out of sympathy with evangelism is absurd. After all, he spent the vast majority of his life trying to convince people of the truth and wonder of the gospel. To do so, he gave up a potentially lucrative career in medicine. What he *was* against was that form of evangelism which is concerned with vast, media-conscious crusades; and what he feared was the tendency in them to man-centred, as opposed to God-centred, evangelism: surely a perfectly valid cautionary note.

As far as 'Deepening of the Spiritual Life conferences' were concerned, it is true that he was not in favour of the so-called 'holiness meetings'. He opposed the notion that the pathway to holiness could be either swift or easy, and in his volume on Ephesians 4:17-5:17 he says this:

> Holiness is not an experience we receive in a meeting. It is to understand that the holy God *hates* sin, the deceitful thing that governs men and gives them lusts and passions. . . . And it is only the man who really knows that, who will hasten to put off the old man and to put on the new

man that after God is created in righteousness and holiness.[18]

Thus holiness to him could only come about as a result of a daily, disciplined process in which the Word of God is of central importance. Surely he was correct to oppose the superficial, glib, short-cut approach to holiness, a corollary to his argument being his awareness of the nature of spirituality:

> The characteristic of spirituality is not glibness, it is reverence, it is holy awe . . . to know God, and if we know Him we know Him to be the holy Father whose name is hallowed.[19]

Cliff's last paragraph, with its implication of the cult of the personality cannot be ignored. Even if one exonerates Lloyd-Jones himself, it is perhaps not easy to excuse the people who bypassed almost empty churches as they travelled to sit at the Doctor's feet in a congregation of 2,000 people. So there is a question of whether − in this sense at least − his ministry may have had a detrimental effect.

The tone of the highly criticial viewpoints outlined above is totally contrasted by Elizabeth Braund's fascinating and unusual recollection of 'the Doctor'. She spent twenty years working with young people in inner-city London, and on one occasion she took a party of boys to North Wales where they found that the other visitors on the farm were 'the Doctor' and Mrs. Lloyd-Jones. It was decided that he would conduct a service in the nearby chapel, which only had a seating capacity for fifty people.

How would these tough, uncompromising boys react to a man widely considered to be an 'intellectual'? For the answer, let Elizabeth Braund tell her own story:

> Wisely, the Doctor explained to the boys that he was going to speak in Welsh to the people for a minute, and after that the service would be in English. The boys sat still, fascinated by the strange sounds, as the Doctor thanked the Welsh people for sharing their service, and reminded

them of where the boys came from. With good will established all round, the meeting continued.

There was spiritual power in the service that night. The Doctor took as his text the story of Paul preaching on Mars Hill, and explained in everyday terms the sort of people who listened to Paul, who their counterparts were today, what he had to say to them, and what it meant for us. There was not a long or complicated word or sentence in the whole sermon, and though the boys sprawled along the pews as they would anywhere else, they listened.

'That was good,' several remarked as they bunched out of the doorway afterwards. Two went further as they walked back to the farm beside me. ' 'E's all right, that bloke. I could understand wot 'e said,' declared one.

'Yeah — it's the first time I ever 'eard anything ter do with religion that made sense,' replied the other.

Another lad joined us and remarked: 'I could 'ear that bloke again. It were interestin' — 'E didn't talk down to us.'[20]

The sequel to this incident too is worth recording:

Some time later an evangelistic team, without any local connections, held a mission near Clapham Junction and visited from house to house for a week in the area. One day I heard an altercation outside the chapel door. Several boys had been approached by the Mission leader and were being given leaflets and urged to attend meetings.

'We got our own,' I heard.

'But there isn't a minister here,' came the answer.

'We got our bloke,' they insisted.

'Who is that?' was the unbelieving query.

'Dr Lloyd-Jones. 'E's orl right.'

I came out to find total astonishment on the leader's face. He would have done better to think carefully about the implications for evangelism of what he had heard.[21]

In the second place, there is the *permanent written legacy* he has left us in the form of books, pamphlets, and lectures. They preserve the distinctives of a long and powerful ministry:

1 His emphasis on the authority of Scripture.[22]
2 His unshakeable view of the importance of preaching for and in the life of the Christian church.[23]
3 His conception and understanding of Christian unity.[24]
4 His *total* confidence in the sufficiency of the gospel to meet human needs at their deepest levels.[25]
5 His stress on the sovereignty of God in history, salvation, the Christian's growth in grace[26], the baptism of the Spirit[27] and the gifts of the Spirit.[28]
6 His clear-cut distinction between evangelism and revival, and the overwhelming need for the latter, which he saw as the 'only hope' for the church.[29]
7 His insistence that Christians are meant to operate as 'salt' and as 'light' in the world.[30]
8 His absolute confidence in the Christian's future hope.[31]

Over a million copies of his books have been sold. If, as seems very likely, they continue to sell in large numbers, they will perpetuate the memory and preaching of a man whose ministry in its total effect has been likened to 'logic on fire'.[32]

The attempt at a critical consensus begun by the Revd. Donald Macleod is surely likely to confirm Dr. R.T. Kendall's view that 'the Doctor' was 'one of the greatest men in the history of the Christian church and without doubt the greatest preacher of the century'.[33]

Bibliography of MLl-J's Works in English[1]

A: *BOOKS (arranged alphabetically)* [2]

1 *The Approach to Faith: Scientific and Religious* (Tyndale Press, 1963).[3]
2 *Authority* (Inter-Varsity Press, 1958).[4]

---

1 Readers who wish to have a bibliography of MLl-J's works published in the Welsh language should consult *Y Cylchgrawn Efengylaidd*, volume 19 number 5, page 40 (Special volume 1981).
2 Numbers 1,2,4,15,31,39, and 40 were not used in the preparation of this study. *Christ our Sanctification* was significant because it challenged the almost total acceptance of 'Keswick' teaching so current among evangelical students at that time, but in later years (most notably in *Joy Unspeakable: The Baptism with the Holy Spirit*) MLl-J admitted that his teaching in *Christ our Sanctification* had been mistaken. Another influential book was *Authority*, published in 1966, which called Christians to recognise the authority of Jesus Christ, of the Scriptures, and of the Holy Spirit. This too was valued by students, especially those who were facing challenges to the authority of Scripture. Its themes are referred to in the body of this study.
3 The dates of the works given are those of the first publication.
4 Re-issued by the Banner of Truth in 1979.

3   *The Basis of Christian Unity* (Inter-Varsity Fellowship, 1962).
4   *Christ our Sanctification* (Inter-Varsity Fellowship, 1948).
5   *The Christian Soldier: An Exposition of Ephesians* 6:10-20
    (Banner of Truth, 1977).
6   *Christian Unity: An Exposition of Ephesians 4:1-16* (Banner
    of Truth, 1980).
7   *The Christian Warfare : An Exposition of Ephesians 6:10-13*
    (Banner of Truth, 1976).
8   *Conversions: Psychological and Spiritual* (Inter-Varsity
    Fellowship, 1959).
9   *Contending for the Faith* (Inter-Varsity Press, 1979).
10 *The Cross: God's Way of Salvation* (Kingsway Publications,
    1986).
11 *Darkness and Light: An Exposition of Ephesians 4:17-5:17*
    (Banner of Truth, 1982).
12 *The Doctor Himself and the Human Condition* (Christian
    Medical Fellowship Publications, 1982).
13 *Evangelistic Sermons at Aberavon* (Banner of Truth, 1983).
14 *Expository Sermons on 2 Peter* (Banner of Truth, 1983).
15 *Faith on Trial: Studies in Psalm 73* (Inter-Varsity Fellowship,
    1973).
16 *From Fear to Faith* (Inter-Varsity Fellowship, 1965).
17 *God's Ultimate Purpose: An Exposition of Ephesians 1*
    (Banner of Truth, 1978).
18 *God's Way of Reconciliation : Studies in Ephesians 2 &*
    (Evangelical Press, 1972).[5]
19 *I am not Ashamed: Advice to Timothy* (Hodder and
    Stoughton, 1986).
20 *Inaugural Address at opening of London Theological
    Seminary* (6th October 1977).
21 Joy Unspeakable: The Baptism with the Holy Spirit
    (Kingway Publications, 1984).
22 *Life in the Spirit: in Marriage, Home and Work: An
    Exposition of Ephesians 5:18-6:9* (Banner of Truth, 1974).

---

5   Re-issued by the Banner of Truth in 1979.

23 *Life's Preparatory School* (Westminster Chapel, ca. 1947/49).

24 *Luther and his Message for Today* (Evangelical Press, 1968).

25 *Maintaining the Evangelical Faith Today* (Inter-Varsity Fellowship, 1952).

26 *The Mirage shall become a Pool* (Westminster Chapel, ca. 1947/49).

27 *The Plight of Man and the Power of God* (Oliphants, 1942).

28 *Preaching and Preachers* (Hodder and Stoughton, 1971).

29 *The Presentation of the Gospel* (Inter-Varsity Fellowship, 1949).

30 *Prove All Things: The Sovereign Work of the Holy Spirit* (Kingsway Publications, 1985).

31 *Roman Catholicism* (Evangelical Press, 1965).

32 *Romans — An Exposition of Chapter 1: The Gospel of God* (Banner of Truth, 1985).

33 *Romans — An Exposition of Chapter 3: 20-4:25: Atonement and Justification* (Banner of Truth, 1970).

34 *Romans — An Exposition of Chapter 5: Assurance* (Banner of Truth, 1971).

35 *Romans — An Exposition of Chapter 6: The New Man* (Banner of Truth, 1972).

36 *Romans — An Exposition of Chapter 7:1-8:4: The Law: its Functions and Limits* (Banner of Truth, 1973).

37 *Romans — An Exposition of Chapter 8:5-17: The Sons of God* (Banner of Truth, 1974).

38 *Romans — An Exposition of Chapter 8:17-39: The Final Perseverance of the Saints* (Banner of Truth, 1975).

39 *1662-1692: from Puritanism to Nonconformity* (Evangelical Library, 1962).

40 *Sound an Alarm* (Westminster Chapel Bookroom, 1957).

41 *Spiritual Depression: its Causes and Cure* (Pickering and Inglis, 1965).

42 *The State of the Nation* (B.E.C. and the Evangelical Press, 1971).

43 *The Supernatural in Medicine* (Christian Medical Fellowship, 1971).
44 *Studies in the Sermon on the Mount 1* (Inter-Varsity Fellowship, 1959).
45 *Studies in the Sermon on the Mount 2* (Inter-Varsity Fellowship, 1960).
46 *Truth Unchanged, Unchanging* (Evangelical Press, 1951).
47 *The Weapons of our Warfare* (Campbell Morgan Memorial Lecture, 1964).
48 *The Unsearchable Riches of Christ: An Exposition of Ephesians 3* (Banner of Truth, 1979).
49 *Why Does God Allow War?* (Hodder and Stoughton, 1939).

B: *PAPERS*

For a list of papers given by MLl-J at the 'Puritan', later Westminster Conferences 1958-78, see *Light from John Bunyan and other Puritans*, pages 103-16.

C: *SELECTIONS FROM MLl-J'S WORKS*

1 *Daily Readings from the Works of Martyn Lloyd-Jones*, Selected by Frank Cumber (Hodder and Stoughton, 1970). Though this is a most useful volume, it was published before the majority if Dr Lloyd-Jones's works appeared.
2 *Light upon the Word: an Anthology of Evangelical Spiritual Writings*, selected and introduced by Herbert Stevenson (Mowbrays, 1979), pages 155-64.

APPENDIX 2

'The Doctor' and the Inter-Varsity Fellowship in Wales

The rise and development of the evangelical student witness in Wales between 1923-83 has been chronicled by the Revd. Geraint Fielder in *Excuse me, Mr. Davies — Hallelujah!* (Evangelical Press of Wales/Inter-Varsity Press, 1983). MLl-J's name occurs frequently in it, and it is clear that his influence on the evangelical unions in the (Welsh) colleges and universities was both considerable and varied.

In the first place, there was the *personal encouragement* he gave. He made his initial visit to University College Cardiff on 7 October 1927, when he spoke on 1 Corinthians 2:2. On this occasion he told his audience that 'university education counts for nothing if we do not believe in Christ'. This statement was all the more impressive because it was not made by a backwoodsman with a bias against higher education, but by a man who had gained his M.D. so early that he had to wait before it could be officially awarded to him.

In the second place, there was — obviously — his *expository preaching*. He was particularly effective in the Welsh I.V.F. conferences. He addressed the first of these, at Pantyfedwen,

Borth, in 1949, on the doctrine of man; the second, at Cilgwyn, Newcastle Emlyn, in 1950, on the Holy Spirit; and the third, at Pantyfedwen again, in 1951, on the Sovereignty of God. Dr. Douglas Johnson has described these series as the best he heard MLl-J deliver, while Geraint Fielder's comment is this: 'Many men look back on these series as being the determining influence on their ministries.' Derek Swann's recollections too are significant:

> When Dr. Lloyd-Jones spoke on the sovereignty of God, *many* of us came to the doctrines of grace for the first time, myself included. He left the doctrine of sovereignty in *salvation* to his last talk, having in the previous two talks laid down all the principles that he would apply in the final talk. I believe the first two talks were on the sovereignty of God in creation and in history. I accepted everything in the first two talks and had eventually to accept them in the third. I remember it was early in the morning in conversation with Gwyn Walters that the truth of election dawned on me. I was so overcome with the wonder of it all that I had to fight back the tears. For many of us since, election has been an affair of the heart as well as the head. I've always been grateful to the Doctor for that. I believe we owe him more than we realize for making it heart-warming stuff (p.157).

Apart from the immediate effects of these conferences in terms of conversions and progress towards a more mature appreciation of Christianity, there were the *longer-term effects* : invigorating 'evangelicalism in the ministry' and giving evangelical life in Wales a new direction in general. Interestingly too, the Welsh evangelical ministers conference grew out of the student conference, leading eventually to the formation of the Evangelical Movement of Wales.

Thirdly, there were MLl-J's *wider gifts*, which went beyond preaching:

R.L. Morgan (a member of University College Cardiff's

evangelical union in the 1920s) remembers the first occasion of many when, instead of giving an address, he invited questions and proceeded to answer them. 'It was a profitable evening and the meeting was of a kind that few people have the confidence or the ability to undertake.' 'Putting questions before long becomes "pelting problems"!' commented another contemporary. 'But Dr. Lloyd-Jones's keen, penetrating mind enables him to see the full implications of a problem and accordingly to guide the discussion with due care.' After one such meeting with a large attendance at the YMCA, the minutes record: 'we realized still more the thoroughness of the testimony of this man of God.' Generations of students in different parts of the world were to experience the bracing rigours of that mind and method, and yet, typically (and uniquely as far as the minutes go), twice comes the comment, 'he made us all feel at home' (p.43).

Reading Fielder's book it is apparent that MLl-J was a tower of strength to Welsh evangelical students. This was particularly true during the 1920s when he encouraged them to look back, for information and enlightenment, to the Reformers, the Puritans, the Calvinistic Methodist fathers, to Spurgeon and to the Princeton Presbyterians. In the late thirties and forties his influence was more pervasive on the Inter-Varsity Fellowship in England than in Wales. But, as Fielder says, most significant for the story of the I.V.F. in Wales is 'the generation of young men and women . . . who were converted to Christ in the forties and fifties . . . who were to respond to the leadership and reflect the ministry of "the Doctor" '. In this sense, therefore, MLl-J's influence is a continuing one.

APPENDIX 3

The Sealing of the Spirit

In developing his argument in *Romans 8:5-17: The Sons of God* MLl-J quotes supporting evidence from a vast array of authorities, including the Puritans John Preston, John Owen, Thomas Horton, and Richard Sibbes, followed later by George Whitefield, John Wesley, the eighteenth-century Methodist Howell Harris, the Americans Jonathan Edwards, Charles G. Finney, Dwight L. Moody, Charles Simeon, the strict Baptist C.H. Spurgeon, and also three great teachers from among the Plymouth Brethren; J.N. Darby, C.H. Mackintosh, and William Kelly.

The evidence he cites is truly massive. This of itself, however, constitutes a problem, for the reader can easily get lost in the wealth of details adduced, quoted and commented on upon. Before coming to the precise implications of the text (Ephesians 1:13, which in the Authorized Versions reads like this: 'In whom ye also trusted, after that ye heard the word of truth, the gospel of your salvation: in whom also after that ye believed, ye were sealed with that Holy Spirit of promise'), it will be of interest to look more closely at the views of one of MLl-J's more surprising witnesses. J.N. Darby (1800-82) was undoubtedly the most gifted teacher amongst the Brethren at the beginning of their history, although his written style is — to say the least — confusing. MLl-J quoted Darby's words accurately, but in order to find out what Darby taught in sources other than the booklet quoted, I turned to Darby's *Letters* for further light on his views and teaching. They contain a number of references to the Sealing of the Spirit.

In 1879, we find Darby holding the same convictions as MLl-J about the nature and effects of the Sealing by the Spirit:

> It is a great truth, a great fact, that the Spirit has been given to us; not only that we are born of the Spirit, but that believing in the efficacy of the blood of Christ, we are sealed with the Holy Spirit; by Him we cry, "Abba, Father"; by Him "the love of God is shed abroad in our hearts"; by Him we know that we are in Christ and that Christ is in us. The work of Christ is the foundation, but the presence of the Holy Ghost is the power of enjoyment. He gives the consciousness that we are children, and heirs, and He is the earnest of our inheritance until the possession of that which Christ has won for us; He causes us to wait for Christ. Once redemption as a personal matter is known, there are the two great truths presented by the word; we have been converted "to wait for his Son from heaven" (1 Thess. i.); and where the Spirit is there is liberty;

Writing in 1881, he clearly distinguishes the new birth from sealing:

> Sealing on the new birth is a mistake in principle; it leaves out the sprinkling with blood for forgiveness. I know of no ground for delay save knowing this. (See Acts ii. 38; x. 43. 44.)

He had made the distinction for some years. In 1871, for example, he wrote:

> *It is true that we are only sealed by the Holy Spirit after having believed.* But it is not then that we are born of God. If the presence of the Holy Spirit were life, every Christian would be an incarnation of the Holy Spirit. Our bodies are temples of the Holy Spirit that we have of God. Being born of God is another thing.

Unlike MLl-J, however, Darby did not believe that a true Christian could remain unsealed. In 1873, he said:

> *But if a man be not sealed, he is not in the christian position: "If any man have not the Spirit of Christ, he is none of his."* Peace through forgiveness is, as to Christ's work, the evidence of faith in Christ's work, and that work received by faith is the ground of sealing: then one is delivered. But the intelligence of this is another thing. Israel, out of Egypt, was brought to God — delivered. Through Jordan they entered in, were circumcised, and ate the corn of the land. But a sealed person alone is in the true christian position; and this is founded on the sprinkling with blood — that is, faith in Christ's work, by which we have redemption, not in the knowledge of deliverance; that is its effect. (My italics).

A year earlier he had said something similar:

> God does not seal an unbeliever, a sinner, in his natural condition. This would be impossible. He will receive such an one in His grace; then He seals him. . . . We are not born again without the Holy Ghost; but His work and his indwelling are two distinct things.

In 1880, he made this forthright statement: 'An unsealed Christian is unknown to Scripture.'

The following comment may indicate some coolness about the whole matter:

> I do not attach especial importance to the immediate moment of the sealing; merely if scripture ascertain it, it is always gain to know it, and I think it does this. I do not think the passages, already presented to me by others, offer any difficulty. Clearly it is because we are sons, that the Spirit is given us to cry Abba, Father, and we are sons by faith of Jesus Christ. But I do not think this passage says anything as to the moment at which, as its occasion, we receive it, but merely states the fact; nor does Ephesians i.

In the last resort, though, what really matter are MLl-J's grammatical and theological arguments, for he takes his stand on a specific reading of Ephesians 1:13, and in particular the phrase 'after that ye believed'. He claims that the underlying verb is past tense:

> It is generally agreed that the Epistle does not say: 'In whom also believing ye *are* sealed with the Holy Spirit.' The word is in the past tense; it is not 'as you believed' or 'when you believed', it is at the very least, 'having believed'. The Revised Version suggests the past, 'having also believed, ye were sealed with the holy Spirit of promise'; and I suggest that even the phrase 'having believed' suggests that these two things are not identical, and that the sealing does not immediately follow the act of belief. What makes this so important is that it is assumed that the sealing with the Spirit, or the baptism with the Spirit, is something which every Christian must of necessity have experienced. It is maintained therefore that this is not something that happens in the realm of consciousness or in the realm of experience, it happens to all believers unconsciously. Therefore they are not to seek it. And the result of not seeking it is that they do not experience it; and the result of that is that they live

in a state of believe-ism, saying to themselves that they must have had it, and therefore do have it. Thus they continue to live without ever experiencing what was experienced by New Testament Christians and also by many other Christians in the subsequent history of the Christian Church. (*Ephesians 1: God's Ultimate Purpose*, pp. 249-50.)

Those evangelicals who disagree with MLl-J call attention to three points. The first of these is grammatical. A literal translation of Ephesians 1:13 would read: 'In whom you also, having heard the word of truth — the gospel of your salvation — in whom also having trusted, you were sealed with that Holy Spirit of promise which is the earnest of our inheritance'. Grammatically 'having heard' and 'having trusted' are exactly parallel: both are aorist participles* and thus must be treated in the same way. Greek often uses the aorist when English uses the present, hence the difference in translation tense. Without a context, the participles could be rendered (a) 'after you believed' (b) 'because you believed' or (c) 'although you believed'. Strictly speaking, therefore, the Greek participle does not indicate a time-lag either negatively or positively. Thus, opponents of MLl-J's views conclude, quite properly, that a temporal argument based on the verb underlying the clause 'after that ye believed' is not admissible.

The second argument is a theological one, namely that the *whole* argument of Ephesians 1:1-14 must be considered. Those who find difficulty with MLl-J indicate that the central proposition is contained in verse 3: that the 'saints' and 'faithful' in Christ have been blessed with 'all' spiritual blessings in Christ Jesus; that the believer has been 'chosen in him', 'predestinated . . . unto the adoption of children', made 'accepted in the beloved', and has had revealed to him the 'mystery of his will', obtained an inheritance, and been given a sure and certain hope for the

---

* F.F. Bruce, *Ephesians* (London, 1961), calls it a 'coincident' aorist because it 'denotes an action coincident in time with that of the main verb' (p.36).

future. Perhaps those who dissent from MLl-J's teaching on this matter concentrate on the fact that salvation is unequivocally Trinitarian: the Father chose us (Eph. 1:4), the Son shed his precious blood for us (Eph. 1:7), and the Holy Spirit sealed us (Eph. 1:13). Also, that Paul gives no hint whatsoever in these verses of a 'two-tier' system whereby there are sealed and unsealed believers. Nor does it suggest that there will be believers in Heaven who have not been sealed, because the only ground of a believer's confidence as far as Heaven is concerned is the possession of the 'Holy Spirit of promise'.

In the third place, attention is drawn to Paul's teaching elsewhere. In Romans 8, Paul puts forward, as indisputable proof of a believer's sonship, the fact that he is led by the 'Spirit of God', and he then underlines the 'Adoption of the Spirit' (8:15-17) in a section that is worth quoting in full:

> For ye have not received the spirit of bondage again to fear; but ye have received the Spirit of adoption, whereby we cry, Abba, Father. The Spirit itself beareth witness with our spirit, that we are the children of God. And if children, then heirs; heirs of God, and joint-heirs with Christ; if so be that we suffer with him, that we may be also glorified together.

This third argument runs as follows: if a man cannot cry 'Abba Father' without the Spirit, if he cannot have any assurance of his sonship without the Spirit, if he cannot be regenerate without the Spirit, then it would be reasonable to assume that when a man becomes a Christian he is given the Holy Spirit (that is, he is sealed) as a proof of authentication of the new life he now possesses in Christ Jesus: it is also proof of his new-found security in Christ Jesus too. Additional and supporting evidence for this third argument is sought in the following passages: John 4:14; 2 Cor. Acts 2:38; 2 Cor. 1:21-22 and 5:5-8; and Colossians 2:9 (where Paul says that we are 'complete in him').

It is ironic that few topics generate so much heat in conservative evangelical circles as the work of the Spirit. MLl-J's assertions were no exception.

APPENDIX 4

Testimony of a Seceder

One of the few clergymen to leave the Church of England was the Revd. Michael Eaton, and here he explains why:

I became a Christian in 1957, through the ministry of an Anglican youth group. This naturally led to my worshipping with my new-found Anglican friends and to my attaching myself to an Anglican parish. When in 1959 I felt called to the Christian ministry it would not have occurred to me to minister in any other denomination than that of the Church of England. Accordingly I went to Tyndale Hall in 1960, remained there as a student during 1960-65, spent an extra year in Tyndale House during 1965-6 and was ordained in Southwark Cathedral in 1966.

During these years, however, I had gradually come to have serious doubts about the distinctives of the Church of England. As a teenager I had read fairly widely and had become aware of the events of 1662, and of the rise of denominations in England especially after 1662. I had read a number of anti-Anglican works by Presbyterians, by Brethren writers, and by the Puritan John Owen. All of them had produced many arguments against the distinctives of Anglicanism that I could not refute. I recall writing a college essay in 1961 about Thomas Hooker and the Puritans in which I argued that the Puritans were right and Hooker wrong. I wrote a book review in the Tyndale Hall student magazine, reviewing *Reformation of the Church*, a rather anti-Anglican collection of historical documents edited by Iain Murray, and reviewed (favourably) by me in 1965.

Another major element — the biggest — in my thinking at that time was the ministry of Dr. Martyn Lloyd-Jones. Someone had recommended that I go and hear him preach and I had gone to listen to him in 1959 when I was a teenager. His message — on Exodus 33 — was greatly moving, and I had its main points fixed on my mind for twenty-five years until I heard it again on cassette tape. Thereafter I periodically tried to get to Westminster Chapel when I could, to hear him. From March 1962 onwards I used to try to get to the Friday night expositions of Romans whenever I could.

One strand of Dr. Lloyd-Jones's ministry was his dislike of Anglicanism and his dislike of ecumenism. I listened and felt convinced by much of what he said. I read his lecture *1662-1962: From Puritanism to Non-Conformity* when it was published in 1962, and his *The Basis of Christian Unity* (1962). I noted his remarks that 'the Anglican church has not known much about revival' (Puritan Studies Conference, 1959, p.39), and his remarks about divisions within Puritanism and its modern relevance (Puritan Studies Conference, 1962). His lecture on *John Owen and Schism* (1963) led me back to the old Puritan arguments. In 1965 I had finished at Tyndale Hall and was preparing to be ordained in October of the following year. In the spring of 1966 Lloyd-Jones' *Ecclesiola in Ecclesia* was published (as one of the Puritan Conference papers) and I again noted his argument that it was not biblical for evangelicals to be a 'wing' of the church or a 'church within a church'. When the Evangelical Alliance meeting of November 1966 took place I had just been ordained yet felt very uncertain about my position in the Church of England. I knew what Lloyd-Jones would say at the meeting in Westminster Central Hall and took a group of young people from my Anglican parish in Surrey to hear him say it. During 1966 Lloyd-Jones had preached through Romans

12:3-8 on Friday evenings and I had heard his expositions
concerning liturgy. Then in early 1967 I heard his expositions
on Romans 13:1-7 and his views concerning the separation of
church and state. I had come to believe in the separation of
church and state and the need of disestablishment of the Church
of England since about 1964(?) when Herbert Carson gave a
lecture on the subject at Tyndale Hall.

At about this time there were three matters that weighed very
heavily with me. They led to my leaving the Church of England
in October 1967.

(i) I had long come to the conclusion that *the concept of a
'state church'* was not really biblical. I had held this conviction
even before I was ordained but had vaguely hoped that one day
the Church of England might be disestablished. Most of my
thinking was done when I was in my teens and early twenties, my
real grasp of the life of the hierarchy of the Church of England was
not very great and most of my thinking was rather doctrinaire
at that time. I had at the time a forlorn hope that disestablishment
would take place. After October 1966 practical parish life threw
me into a very different world from my student life in Bristol
and Cambridge, and made the matters I had thought about
theoretically a matter of daily reality. The 'state church' side
of the matter now troubled me in real existence. I would be
compelled to marry couples who seemed to have no Christian
faith. Sometimes bridegrooms would arrive for the service
having had rather too much to drink on the way. At funerals one
had to declare that all and sundry died 'with sure and certain
hope' regardless of their previous faith or lack of it. At baptisms
of children (in which I still believed) one had to declare that
the children were regenerate. I only once took such a service
and had an experience rather like that of Luther at his first Mass!
All of this tied in with a 'state church' and was taking place at
the same time as I was listening to Lloyd-Jones on Romans 13.
I remembered Richard Hooker's statement that every member
of the commonwealth (i.e. of the nation) was a member of the
Church of England, and knew that I could not survive much
longer. For I knew that I radically disagreed with Hooker's
viewpoint.

(ii) I was very unhappy with the *enforced ecumenism* of the Church of England. I had heard for several years Lloyd-Jones' arguments against evangelicals being a 'wing' of the church, and the need of visible unity of evangelicals, and the weakness of an *ecclesiola in ecclesia.* I would not have minded so much if I had been free to hold my own viewpoint while knowing that most of the Church of England held a different one. What put practical pressures on me was that I was constantly forced into situations where I seemed to be confessing a faith that I did not believe. I had, for example, to take part in the 'Mass' at the Clergy School of Southwark diocese. The chaplain at a local Anglican school seemed to have no Christian faith at all, yet he and I were often forced to share a joint platform, and young people were puzzled that we preached such diametrically opposite gospels. I felt I was constantly being *forced* to support versions of the Christian gospel which I did not believe in. The suffragan bishop at the time was John Robinson whose version of Christianity was popular with some young Anglican curates. I did not feel that I worshipped the same God or shared the same faith as theirs, yet I was in the same denominational set-up. It led to contradictions which I felt compromised the gospel I believed in.

(iii) I was unhappy with *the liturgical aspect* of the Church of England. I enjoyed preaching but did not enjoy Prayer Book worship. This had been a problem for me for years. I had loved Tyndale Hall and had been blissfully happy there in every aspect except College Chapel. Daily Prayer Book worship had been a torment for me (I often skipped it!) I had hoped I would manage to take some liberties with the Prayer Book in practice, but found I did not have the freedom I hoped. I felt the strength of Owen and Lloyd-Jones' arguments that *imposition* of liturgical worship was retrograde. (Mind you, Lloyd-Jones did not contrast liturgy versus free worship; he contrasted any 'mere' praying with praying in the Spirit.)

In each of these matters, Dr. Lloyd-Jones had considerable influence. Although he never put the slightest pressure on me to leave the Church of England, when I went to see him about them in October 1967 he heartily agreed with what I was saying, and encouraged me in what I had already determined — that my days in the Church of England were finished.

What *precipitated* my leaving the Church of England was conflict with Mervyn Stockwood.* If that had not arisen I probably would have stayed nominally Anglican but would have moved inconspicuously into freer interdenominational ministry. In the event I quarrelled with Mervyn Stockwood at the time of my 'priesting', decided there was no future for me in the Church of England, went to see Lloyd-Jones, and never ministered in an Anglican church again.

In the 1960s it was easier to talk about secession than actually to secede. Many of my contemporaries in the 1960s talked about secession, but in practice one had so many ties with friends, and one's emotional ties were such that secession was not so easy — psychologically — as one might suppose. Had Mervyn Stockwood not given me an extra push I doubt whether I could ever have brought myself to leave the Church of England. Many of my contemporaries who held views identical to my own did not secede, even men who had earnestly talked about doing so. It appears that in actual practice few people ever secede from a denomination they have spiritually grown up in, unless something happens that gives them a push or an unexpected opportunity arises that makes a change easier. This is what happened to me. Lloyd-Jones gave me a theological rationale for freechurchmanship; Mervyn Stockwood virtually threw me out of the Church of England, but I was happy to go. Many of my contemporaries held similar views but did not get the extra push.

* Bishop of Southwark.

Notes

CHAPTER ONE

1 See *Preaching and Preachers* (Hodder and Stoughton, 1971), p.9, 'The Primacy of Preaching'.
2 See *Preaching and Preachers*, p.9.
3 The full version of this letter is found in chapter two.
4 Chapter four deals with the main areas of controversy in his life.
5 *The Evangelical Magazine of Wales* (April 1981), pp. 45-47.
6 *D. Martyn Lloyd-Jones: The First Forty Years 1899-1939* (The Banner of Truth Trust, 1982).
7 This is how Dr. Lloyd-Jones was invariably referred to both in Aberavon and at Westminster Chapel, and often in general amongst Evangelicals. In this study we shall ring the changes, using 'he', 'the Doctor', and 'MLl-J'.
8 The letter is dated '10th January 1973'. It was type-written, ends 'Yours very sincerely', followed by MLl-J's own handwritten signature.

CHAPTER TWO

1 For those desiring a historical perspective, this is the relevant information: Marquis of Salisbury (1895-1902), A.J. Balfour (1902-05), Henry Campbell-Bannerman (1905-08), H.H. Asquith (1908-16), David Lloyd-George (1916-22), A. Bonar Law (1922-23), Stanley Baldwin (1923, 1924, 35-37), J.R. Macdonald (1924, 29-35), Neville Chamberlain (1937-40), Winston Churchill (1940-45, 51-55), Clement Attlee (1945-51), Anthony Eden (1955-57), Harold Macmillan (1957-63), Alex Douglas Home (1963), Harold Wilson (1964-70, 74-76), Edward Heath (1970-74), Jim Callaghan (1976-79), Margaret Thatcher (1979-83, 1983 and onwards).
2 See Murray's Introduction to *D. Martyn Lloyd-Jones: The First Forty Years 1899-1939*, pp. xi-xv.
3 It is estimated that a million copies of his books had been sold by the end of 1983.

4 See Murray, op.cit., p.3.
5 *Sir Thomas Horder (1871-1955)* – educated at St. Bartholomew's
   Hospital; M.B., B.S. London, 1898; M.D., 1899; member of the
   Royal College of Physicians in London, 1899; Fellow of the Royal
   College of Physicians, 1906; an outstanding clinician, his patients
   included King George V, King George VI, and Queen Elizabeth
   II. Knighted in 1918, created a Baronet in 1923, and a Baron ten
   years later. See *Dictionary of National Biography*, pp. 501-3. Clearly
   it was an honour for MLl-J to have been noticed by Horder.
6 Murray, op.cit., p.53-4.
7 *Preaching and Preachers*, p.146.
8 Murray, op.cit., p.77.
9 Which says 'To the one we are the savour of death unto death; and
   to the other a savour of life unto life. And who is sufficient for these
   things?'
10 Murray, op.cit., p.110.
11 *Memories of Sandfields 1927-38* (The Banner of Truth Trust, 1983),
   p.10.
12 The services at Sandfields were for the most part traditional:
   preaching services on Sunday at 11am and 6pm, Prayer Meeting on
   Monday evening, Fellowship meeting on Wednesday evening, with
   a 'Brotherhood' meeting for men on Saturday evening. Other
   activities such as the football team, the drama group, and the 'Band
   of Hope' (essentially a temperance movement) were all got rid of.
13 *Evangelistic Sermons at Aberavon* (The Banner of Truth Trust, 1983),
   p.76-7.
14 Ibid., p.199.
15 Ibid., p.142.
16 *Memories*, p.12-15.
17 Ibid., pp. 66-79.
18 See ibid., pp. 80-94.
19 See Murray, op.cit., p.183.
20 See chapter three.
21 *Evangelistic Sermons*, pp. 269-70.
22 Ibid., p.273.
23 Ibid., pp. 274-5.
24 Ibid., pp. 277-78.
25 Ibid., p.279.
26 Ibid., p.25.
27 *Evangelical Magazine of Wales* (April 1981), p.34.
28 *Memories*, p.95.
29 Ibid., p.96.
30 Quoted in *LINK* (a magazine of the Godalming Council of Churches)
   August 1970.
31 *Preaching and Preachers*, pp. 302-3.
32 Ibid., p.300.

33 See ibid., p.63.
34 *Evangelical Times* (April 1981), p.10.
35 Murray, op.cit., 'Introduction', p.xiii.
36 *Evangelical Magazine of Wales* (April 1981), p.43.
37 *Evangelistic Sermons*, p.48.
38 Ibid., p.50.
39 Ibid., p.51.
40 Published 3 March 1981.
41 See Murray, op.cit., p.228.
42 See ibid., p.130.

CHAPTER THREE

1 *Expository Sermons on 2 Peter* (The Banner of Truth Trust, 1983), p.135.
2 *Studies In The Sermon On The Mount* (I.V.F. reprint, 1966), volume 1 (Matthew 5), p.vii.
3 *Romans 3:20-4:25: Atonement and Justification* (The Banner of Truth Trust, 1970), p.xii.
4 *Preaching and Preachers* (Hodder and Stoughton, 1971), pp. 97-8.
5 *Romans 8:5-17: The Sons of God* (The Banner of Truth Trust, 1974), p.47.
6 *The Plight Of Man And The Power Of God* (Pickering and Inglis reprint, 1966), p.32.
7 *Evangelical Times* (April 1981), p.9.
8 *Sound An Alarm* (Westminster Chapel Bookroom, 1957), p.4.
9 *Expository Sermons on 2 Peter*, p.157.
10 *Ephesians 4:10-16: Christian Unity* (The Banner of Truth Trust, 1980), pp. 13-14.
11 *Faith on Trial* (I.V.F., 1965), 'Preface'.
12 *Romans 3:20-4:25: Atonement and Justification*, p.159.
13 *Evangelistic Sermons at Aberavon* (The Banner of Truth Trust, 1983), p.153.
14 *Ephesians 4:10-16: Christian Unity*, p.49. This comment is part of MLl-J's treatment of verses 4-6.
15 *Ephesians 4:10-16: Christian Unity*, pp. 13-14.
16 *Evangelistic Sermons*, pp. 63-64.
17 *Studies In The Sermon On The Mount*, volume 1, p.153.
18 Ibid., p.155.
19 *Evangelical Times* (April 1981), p.10.
20 *Preaching and Preachers*, p.305.
21 *Evangelical Times* (April 1981), p.14.
22 The acronym TULIP stands for: Total Depravity of Man, Unlimited Election, Limited Atonement, Irresistible Grace, Perseverance of the Saints.

23 *Dedication* (May-June 1981), p.22.
24 *Evangelical Times* (April 1981), p.18.
25 In 1977 he made his fiftieth consecutive yearly visit there.
26 See chapter 17 of Murray's biography.
27 *Evangelical Times* (April 1981), p.14.
28 *Contending for the Faith* (Inter-Varsity Press, 1979), p.185.
29 Ibid., p.233.
30 See Appendix on ' "The Doctor" and the Inter-Varsity Fellowship in Wales'.
31 *Preaching and Preachers*, p.126.

CHAPTER FOUR

1 *Preaching and Preachers* (Hodder and Stoughton, 1971), p.267.
2 Ibid., p.267.
3 Ibid., pp. 272-73.
4 Ibid., p.282.
5 Ibid., p.282.
6 Herbert Carson, in *Evangelical Times* (April 1981), says: 'But in the atmosphere of 1954-55 there was no possibility of being silent or neutral. You were forced to say what your attitude was to mass evangelism. Indeed, it almost became a touchstone of evangelical orthodoxy. One indignant evangelical leader even queried the IVF for having a man like Lloyd-Jones as a Vice-President; since he did not support the crusade'. He goes on to say, quite properly, that such an independent stance cost MLl-J a great deal.
7 See J. Elwyn Davies, *Striving Together: The Evangelical Movement of Wales — its principles and aims* (Evangelical Press of Wales, 1984), pp. 8-9.
8 *Evangelical Magazine of Wales* (April 1981), p.41.
9 See Appendix 5.
10 See Murray, op.cit., pp. 194-5.
11 In his *Foreword* to Eifion Evans's *The Welsh Revival of 1904*, 'the Doctor' says: 'it is essential that Christians should be clear as to the difference between revival and organized evangelism'.

CHAPTER FIVE

1 This is the Authorized Version rendering.
2 The Revd. McMillan very kindly sent me his views in a most comprehensive letter dated August 1984.
3 I am grateful to Pastor Rodwell for his letters to me, and for the loan of letters from MLl-J to him.
4 Two of them are worth reproducing here, both written from 39,

Mount Park Crescent, Ealing, London W5. The first is dated 16 March 1961:

> My Dear Friend,
> How delighted we were to receive your letter this morning and to hear the good news that you are settled happily in the work in Huntingdonshire. This sounds an ideal arrangement and I am sure that you are going to be very happy in it, especially when Mrs Rodwell finds something suitable. I am sure that you have only to keep within the limits prescribed for you and all will be well. It was very good of you to let us know.
> We shall never forget your great kindness during that terrible period in 1944.
> With much love from us all to you all.
> Yours very sincerely,
> D.M. Lloyd-Jones

An earlier letter, dated 2 April 1960, is in similar vein:

> My dear Friend,
> Though we met the other day I feel I must send just a word to tell you how delighted I was to see you once more and to have a brief word with you. It is always a joy to meet you and it always brings back happy memories of our association now over a number of years.
> I am glad, as I told you, to hear something of what has been happening to you, though sorry to hear that you have been having such a difficult time. However, it was good to see that in spite of all the buffetings you were still your old self, full of faith, courage and hope. As always, it did me great good to see you.
> May God continue to bless you all as a family. My wife joins with me in sending warmest love to you all.
> Yours very sincerely,
> D.M. Lloyd-Jones

CHAPTER SIX

1 See *Westminster Record* (Memorial Number, June 1981), p.463.
2 See *Preaching and Preachers*, pp. 172, 179-80, 182-83.
3 Published in the *Westminster Record* (Memorial Number, June 1981), p.473.
4 In the Authorized Version these verses read as follows: 'Be careful for nothing; but in every thing by prayer and supplication with thanksgiving let your requests be made known unto God. And the

peace of God, which passeth all understanding, shall keep your hearts and minds through Christ Jesus.'

5 See *Evangelical Times* (April 1981), where, on page 9, MLl-J's letter to Mr. Geoffrey Williams offering him support is printed in full.

6 See *The Monthly Record of the Free Church of Scotland* (February 1984), p.43.

7 *The Plight of Man And The Power Of God* (Oliphants, 1942), pp. 82-83.

8 *From Fear to Faith* (I.V.F., 1953), p.73.

9 Part of Mr. Keith Newell's letter to me dated 4 June 1984.

10 See Victor Budgen, *On Fire For God: The Story of Jan Huss* (Evangelical Press, 1983), p.63.

11 *Ephesians 1:1-23: God's Ultimate Purpose* (Banner of Truth Trust, 1978), p.92.

12 A fuller version of Professor Collins's views is found in chapter five.

13 This viewpoint was communicated to me in a letter dated August 1984.

14 Part of a letter from Mrs. Helen Bradbury, Hastings, July 1984.

15 In a letter from John Davies, Warwickshire, dated 3 July 1984.

16 Another part of the letter from Mr. Keith Newell.

17 A submission by Mr. Norman Cliff, Colchester, Essex.

18 *Ephesians 4:17-5:17: Darkness and Light* (Banner of Truth Trust, 1982), p.186.

19 *Ephesians 4:17-5:17*, p.185.

20 This story is found in Elizabeth Braund's book, *The Young Woman Who Lived In a Shoe* (Marshall Pickering, 1984).

21 *Ibid.*

22 See *Expository Sermons on 2 Peter* (Banner of Truth Trust, 1983), p.212.

23 See *Studies In The Sermon On The Mount* (I.V.F., 1959), volume 1, p.vii.

24 See *Ephesians 4:1-16: Christian Unity* (Banner of Truth Trust, 1980).

25 See *The Doctor Himself and the Human Condition* (Christian Medical Fellowship Publications), p.14.

26 See *From Fear to Faith* (I.V.F., 1965), p.22.

27 *Joy Unspeakable: The Baptism with the Holy Spirit* (Kingsway Publications, 1984).

28 *Prove All Things: The Sovereign Work of the Holy Spirit* (Kingsway Publications, 1985).

29 See *Foreword* to *The Welsh Revival of 1904* (Evangelical Press of Wales, 1984), by Eifion Evans, p.5.

30 See *Studies In The Sermon On The Mount*, volume 1, pp. 148ff.

31 See *Ephesians 1*, p.445.

32 See Christopher Catherwood, *Five Evangelical Leaders* (Hodder and Stoughton, 1984), pp. 51-109.

33 From a letter to me dated 16 May 1984.